ORIC-1

Basic
Programming
Manual

First Published in the United Kingdom
by Sunshine Publications

This Remastered Edition
Published in 2022 by
ACORN BOOKS
acornbooks.uk

This book is a page-by-page reproduction of the original 1983 edition as published by Sunshine Publications. The entirety of the book is presented with no changes, corrections nor updates to the original text, images and layout; therefore no guarantee is offered as to the accuracy of the information within.

ORIC-1

Basic
Programming
Manual

by **John Scriven**

Contents

CHAPTER 1
Introduction

1. Introduction

Congratulations! You are the possessor of one of the most advanced micro-computers available today. This book will be required reading to those of you who have never used a computer before. It will also be useful to anyone coming from other systems, as ORIC has many features that make it more powerful than other machines. If you are used to computers, you may find it easier to skip through the next chapter.

You will learn a lot from reading the manual, but you will only become proficient by using ORIC frequently. We hope that you will find it a friendly computer that will become the heart of an expanding system. You will soon discover about ORIC's 'drivability'. Even beginners will find computing is easy with ORIC.

CHAPTER 2
Setting the Computer up

2. Setting the Computer Up

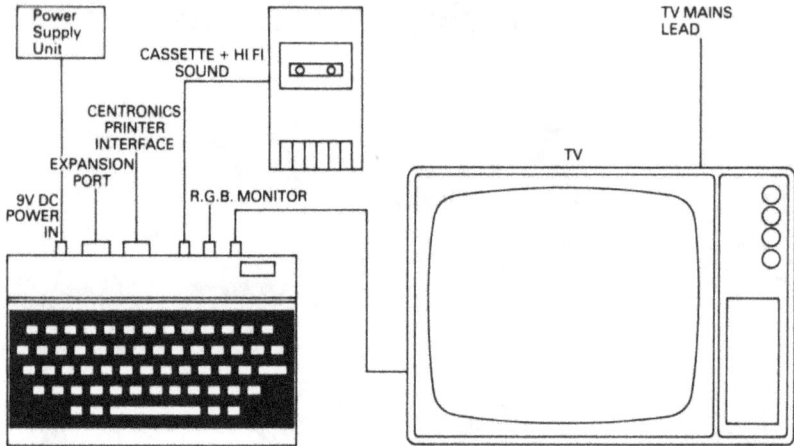

When you unpack your ORIC, you will notice that it has a keyboard, to enter information, and several sockets at the back. It needs these to communicate with the outside world. First of all, connect the power supply according to the instructions on the lead and push the small plug into the socket at the back. ORIC only needs a low D.C. voltage so never plug it directly into the mains.

The keyboard provides an input, but you will not see the results of any key presses unless you plug it into a T.V. Using the connecting lead, plug one end in the back of ORIC and the other end to the U.H.F. aerial socket on your T.V. Most T.V.'s purchased in the last 15 years will operate satisfactorily, although a black and white T.V. will only give you shades of grey.

Now the moment you've been waiting for — switch on the mains, and tune your T.V. to approximately Channel 36. If you have a rotary tuner, this won't be difficult: otherwise tune in a spare button. When you are in the right place, you should see the following picture on your T.V.

```
ORIC EXTENDED BASIC V1.0
© 1983 TANGERINE
x   BYTES FREE
READY
```

If you look at the back of ORIC you will see some other sockets. The setting-up diagram shows you their particular function. Some of them will be useful fairly soon, some will be used as you expand your system.

The most important socket is for the cassette recorder. Almost any make will do — cheap portables are better than expensive hi-fi models. When you type in a program and want to save it, ORIC will turn it into a sound signal that can be recorded. This can be reloaded whenever you wish and you won't need to type it again!

You need a lead with a three or seven pin DIN plug on one end, and either a DIN plug or 3.5mm jack plugs on the other, according to the sockets on your recorder.

Next to the cassette socket is the R.G.B. colour monitor socket. The signal that comes out of ORIC, through the T.V. socket, has to be coded into a U.H.F. signal for your television set, which then decodes it. A monitor is like a T.V. set without the sound and tuning section. If you use ORIC with a monitor you'll get an even better picture. The signal does not have to be encoded and decoded.

If you want to make a permanent record of what ORIC prints on the screen, you can connect a printer via the next socket. To make it easier, most manufacturers make printers that use standard plugs. ORIC will connect to any printer that has a Centronics interface.

The last socket is the largest, and provides ways of connecting up ORIC to many other pieces of equipment.

Some examples are:— extra memory, games cartridges, joysticks and, of course, the modem. This device will allow ORIC to download PRESTEL pages, or even programs, and to send and receive electronic mail via the PRESTEL MAILBOX system.

Underneath ORIC is a little button that you may need a pencil to operate. This is a **RESET** button and is an emergency device to get you out of never ending loops. It does not switch off the power but only stops execution of a program. It could also be referred to as a *warm start* button, as it does not destroy the contents of the memory.

FINE TUNING THE COLOUR PICTURE

Before your Oric left the factory it was tuned to send a perfect signal to our test television. Television sets differ from model to model, however, and you may like to fine tune the picture. You should do this if there is any indication of a slight waviness on the edge of the picture or if the yellow in the colour band is a bit washed out.

To fine tune your Oric leave it switched on and turn it over. On the bottom you will see a large hole (number 1 in the diagram below) and a small hole (number 2)

TUNING THE PICTURE

Inside hole (1) there is a small recess into which you can put the tip of a very small screw driver. Insert your screw driver and *very gently* move the socket ⅛ of a turn to the left, back to the centre and then an ⅛ turn to the right. Adjust the picture to the best position.

TUNING THE COLOUR

Inside hole (2) there is a small brass screw for fine tuning the colour. Turn it *very gently* for a fraction of a turn in each direction to find the best result.

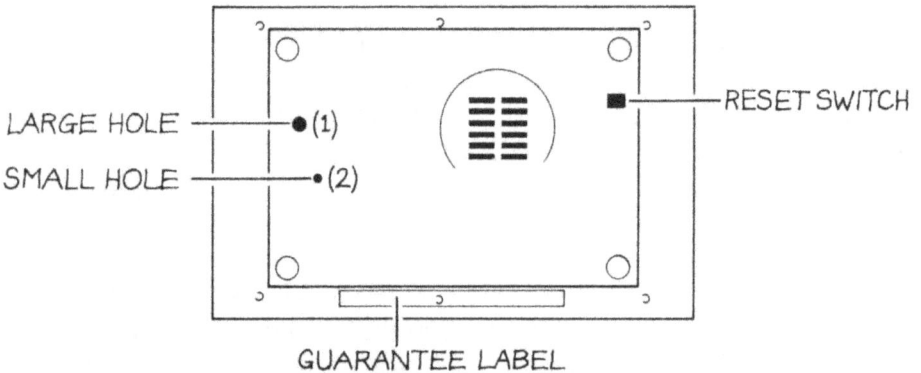

LARGE HOLE ———— ●(1)

SMALL HOLE ———— ●(2)

RESET SWITCH

GUARANTEE LABEL

CHAPTER 3
Programming in Basic

3. Programming in BASIC

First the bad news — ORIC doesn't understand English. But now the good news — you don't have to learn a complicated electronic language, because ORIC speaks a language called BASIC, (Beginners All-purpose Symbolic Instruction Code). This language was invented in 1964 to help people to write computer programs easily. If your machine is switched on, we'll see how easy this is.

Type

PRINT "HELLO"

and then press the [*RETURN*] key.

As you typed the letters in they should have appeared on the screen and, when you pressed [*RETURN*], the word **HELLO** should have appeared just under it. The flashing square is called the cursor. It tells you where the words appear on the screen. **PRINT** is a BASIC command, yet it means the same as it does in English. Try **PRINT**ing some other things on the screen. Remember to put quotation marks round what you want to say and don't forget to press [*RETURN*].

Now enter

WRITE "HELLO"

and press [*RETURN*].

Oops! You've just been given an error message. The words

? SYNTAX ERROR

means you've made a mistake. Although BASIC is easy to learn, and close to English, you must use the correct words or ORIC won't understand.

A peek inside the ORIC may help to clarify things a little. Inside ORIC, there are several microchips. The most important one is the C.P.U. (Central Processor Unit) which is ORIC's brain. Microchips use high or low voltages to work. If you imagine a row of eight light-bulbs with switches underneath, then you can see that any of them can be on or off. You can think of the chips as all containing lots and lots of these eight block switches. Each switch is called a bit, and each block is called a byte.

If you think about it, there are 256 different combinations of ons and offs. If on = 1 and off = Ø then this is one way to store 256 numbers. This system is called binary.

Binary		*Normal decimal*
00000000	=	0
00000001	=	1
00000010	=	2
00000011	=	3
00000100	=	4
etc.		
11111110	=	254
11111111	=	255

This is why some people think of computers as being only to do with maths − in fact, the zeros and ones can stand for letters, or words, or almost anything. This is similar to the way morse code can say anything it likes using only dots and dashes.

Another important chip in ORIC is the BASIC ROM (Read Only Memory). This translates words in BASIC into zeros and ones that ORIC's brain can understand. There are not very many BASIC words, somewhere between one and two hundred. There are several different versions of BASIC around, just as there are several different versions of English.

For example, English spoken in London is not quite the same as that spoken in New York. If a Londoner talks about the pavement, he means what an American would call the sidewalk. This is why we have to speak correctly to ORIC, or else we will be given error messages.

Type

PRINT "5"

then [*RETURN*], then type

PRINT 5

then [*RETURN*] Apparently, there's no difference.
Now type

PRINT "5 + 2"

then type

PRINT 5 + 2

(By now you should be used to pressing [*RETURN*] key, so I'll stop reminding you.) If you enter information in quotes, it's called a *string,* and *strings* can be letters, numbers, even graphics characters!

If you enter information without quotes, then ORIC assumes it's a number, and if it's in the form of a sum, it will work out the answer for you.

Try

PRINT 75 + 25

You should get **1Ø0**. *Hint* — you can type ? instead of **PRINT** to save time. (notice the difference between a zero -Ø- and a capital O, and between one -1- and a capital I — you know which is meant, but ORIC has to be told correctly).

Try other calculations. The subtract key is next to Ø, divide is / and multiply is * (shift 8).

If you make a mistake , press **CTRL** key and **X**. A backslash will appear and the whole line will be deleted.

If you're interested in more complicated maths, remember that ORIC does not operate on numbers as they arrive.

PRINT 4 + 3*2 will not give you **14**, but **10** because * is more important than + . Here is the order of priority, most important at the top, least important at the bottom.

```
()
 ↑         ("to the power of")
*,/
+,-
```

Operators on the same line have the same priority. This is a way of using ORIC as a calculator.
Enter these examples so you understand about priorities.

PRINT 2*3*4
PRINT 4 + 3*2
PRINT 4*3 + 2
PRINT 4/2 + 3
PRINT 2 + 3/4
PRINT 3 + 4↑2
PRINT 3 – 4↑2
PRINT 2 + 4↑3*2

If you are uncertain then put the part of the argument (equation) you want calculated first in brackets. e.g.

4 + 3*2 = 10

but

(4 + 3)*2 = 14

* * * * * * * * *

Do you remember I said that ORIC assumed everything without quotes was a number?

11

Type
PRINT H

and see what happens You should get a Ø. Of course it can't be a number — or can it? Type

LET H = 4

Now type
PRINT H

This time ORIC knows that you've set **H** equal to **4** (just like in algebra). **H** is called a *variable*. ORIC will remember this until you either change the value of **H**, or type **CLEAR**, or switch off. Try this with other letters, then type **CLEAR** and see if ORIC has forgotten them. You can use more than one letter, so **AB** could have a different value to **A** or **B**. You can also have **A5** or **A6**. ORIC will accept *variables* of more than two characters in length, but will only recognize the first two.
Try:—

LET JOHN = 36
LET JOCELYN = 28

Now type

PRINT JOHN
PRINT JOCELYN

You should get **28** each time, because ORIC has only remembered a *variable* **JO**, which although originally set to **36**, was reset to **28**. Enter

PRINT 4*JO

and you can see how *variables* can be treated just like ordinary numbers. So far we have only dealt with numbers. How can ORIC remember names? Just as there are numbers and also number *variables*, there are *strings* and *string variables*.
Type

LET N$ = "BLAKE"

Now type

PRINT N$

12

You should see that **"BLAKE"** has been remembered as a *string variable*. Try to set **FP$** to your favourite person's name. If you type

PRINT N$, FP$

you should get both names on the screen. The comma sets a space between the *strings*, like using **TAB** on a typewriter. ORIC has **TAB** settings five characters apart. If you use a semi-colon(;) there is no gap between variables. e.g.

PRINT N$;FP$

It is possible to add *strings* together to make a new *string*. Type

LET A$ = N$ + FP$

then **PRINT A$**. This is called concatenation. Try using **CLEAR** again to check if it clears *string variables* too.

Note:— You don't have to use **LET** to assign values to *variables*. i.e. **A = 10** is the same as **LET A = 10** to ORIC.

When we were talking about *number variables*, you probably discovered that decimal fractions could be held in *variables*, as well as whole numbers.

Try:

LET X = 1/3
PRINT X

You should get **0.333333333**

(ORIC can hold numbers between 2.93874×10^{-39} up to 1.70141×10^{38}). For further explanation see Chapter 6.

Simple letters should be called *floating point variables*. If the letter, or pair of letters, is followed by a % then it is called an *integer* or *whole number variable* e.g. **A% = 4762**. These can be between -32768 and $+32767$. In general *integer variables* can be handled faster than *floating point variables*.

So far, we've only used ORIC to give us results in a simple way. This is called *immediate execution* or *calculator* mode. The usual way to use computers is to get them to store a sequence of instructions and to use this *program* when we require.

In BASIC, the order of actions is controlled by line numbers. It is usual to set the line numbers 10 apart so extra lines can be inserted later. It doesn't matter in which order you enter the lines. ORIC will sort them into the correct order automatically.

Try this short program.

```
10   CLS
20   PRINT "ENTER YOUR NAME"
30   INPUT N$
40   PRINT "PLEASED TO MEET YOU , ";N$
```

ORIC will go to the first line number, 10 and clear the screen, **PRINT** "Enter your name" and then go to line 30. This says **INPUT N$**, so the program will halt here until you enter something and type [*RETURN*]. N$ now contains your name. ORIC will leap to line 40 and print

"PLEASED TO MEET YOU"

followed by your name. The semi-colon (;) prints your name after it. Semi-colons are not necessary in **PRINT** statements but may make the listing clearer. They suppress the line-feed so be careful about putting them at the end of lines. Type **RUN**. This sets the program into operation from the lowest line number — it also clears any *variables* previously set, so you can keep running the program with different names.

Although it's not necessary with ORIC, it's usual to put **END** as the last line of the program.

Type **LIST** and your program will scroll neatly up the screen. Now add these lines.

```
 50   PRINT "ENTER THE YEAR IN WHICH YOU WERE
       BORN"
 60   INPUT YEAR
 70   LET AGE = 1983 — YEAR
110   PRINT "YOU MUST BE ABOUT ";AGE;" YEARS
       OLD ";N$
120   GOTO 200
200   END
```

If you make a mistake in a line you can delete the whole line by simply entering the line number. Try typing **60** then **LIST**ing the program. Retype **60 INPUT YEAR**. Now **RUN** the program.

* * * * * * * * *

DECISIONS

So far we've used the computers to work through all the numbers without making any decisions. Let's use ORIC's brain a little more. Add these lines. (Feminists may wish to alter the wording of lines 80 + 150!)

```
80  PRINT "EXCUSE MY ASKING, BUT ARE YOU
    FEMALE ";N$; " (Y/N)?"
90  INPUT A$
100 IF A$ = "Y" THEN 150
150 PRINT "WELL, "N$" AN ATTRACTIVE GIRL LIKE
    YOU MUST BE ABOUT 18"
```

Line 100 contains a conditional branch. A$ should be either "Y" or "N". ORIC tests to see if A$ = "Y". If this assertion is true **THEN** the program jumps to line 150. If this assertion is false, i.e. if anything else has been entered, then the program continues to the next line, prints the age, and then stops. See the end of this chapter for a discussion on the use of **ELSE**.

You will probably see that the program only tests for "Y" as a reply. "OK" or "YEAH" or "JUST ABOUT" would be counted as not "Y" and therefore false — so be warned, although ORIC is very good at obeying instructions, these must be specified carefully in the first place.

You might like to try to alter line 100 to cope with other answers. You can start with

```
100 IF A$ = "Y" OR A$ = "YES" OR A$ = "YUP"
    THEN 150
```

Up till now all you've been printing has been in capitals. You've probably discovered that **SHIFT** doesn't seem to work.

If you press **CTRL** and **T** at the same time you'll find ORIC'S keyboard acts like a typewriter — lower case (small letters) normally and upper case (capitals) when you hold **SHIFT** down at the same time. If you press control T (**CTRL** and **T**) ORIC will go back to using capitals only. To let you know you're in CAPS mode, ORIC prints CAPS on the status line at the top of your screen.

There is a lot of sense in this. If you type **run** in small letters, you'll get

? SYNTAX ERROR

All BASIC commands and variables must be in capitals.

You can type anything into ORIC and press any of the keys and you will not harm the computer. The worst that can happen is that you get into an endless loop or you manage to corrupt the screen — if anything strange happens to the screen, first press **RESET**. If nothing happens, switch off the mains, wait a few seconds and power up again. You will get the initial screen picture. ORIC will not complain, but you might, if you have to re-type your program!

What happens when you grow fed up with a program and want to get rid of it? Instead of switching off, you can simply type **NEW**. This will clear the memory and set all *variables* to zero.

** * * * * * * *

LOOPS

ORIC has shown us so far that computers are capable of making decisions according to whether conditions are true or false. They are also capable of repeating an action for however many times you require.

For instance, if you want ORIC to print all the numbers from 1 to 1000 and scroll them up the side of the screen, you could type:—

```
10    PRINT 1
20    PRINT 2
30    PRINT 3
40    PRINT 4
```

But you'd get rather fed up doing this 1000 times! Luckily there is a BASIC command called the **FOR....TO/NEXT** loop, that will repeat an instruction whilst it counts to itself until the final number is reached.

This is how it works:—

```
10    FOR X = 1 TO 1000 STEP 1
20    PRINT X
30    NEXT X
40    PRINT "PHEW! THAT'S FINISHED".
```

Line 10 sets the counter **X** to 1, then goes to line 20. There it prints **X**, which is 1, and then goes to 30. This says **NEXT X**, so it shoots back to the start of the loop at line 10 and increases it by the **STEP** number (i.e. **X** is now 2). It prints **X** in line 20 then repeats as before until **X** is 1000. This time it tries to make **X** = 1001, but it has been told to only go up as far as 1000, so it jumps to the next line — 40, where it prints

"FINISHED".

If you change the **STEP** number to 2, then it will print **1,3,5,7** etc. You can leave it out, and ORIC will assume you want a **STEP** size of 1.

Try other **STEP** sizes yourself.

FOR/NEXT loops can count backwards, but you have to specify the **STEP** number as a negative quantity.

```
10    FOR X = 1000 TO 1 STEP -1
```

will count downwards.

If you make a mistake in the numbers, e.g.

FOR X = 4 TO 2 STEP 5

or
FOR X = 5 TO 100 STEP -1

17

then the action in the loop will still be performed at least once, because the test for whether the loop is completed is not made until the loop has reached the **NEXT** statement and returned to the start.

Another use for **FOR/NEXT** loops is as a pause. You probably found that ORIC prints so fast that you couldn't see the numbers. To slow it down, we can put in

25   FOR PAUSE = 1 TO 100: NEXT PAUSE

This is like saying "Count up to 100 each time you print a number, then continue". Note the use of a colon to achieve two statements in one line.

Be careful about using this facility if there is an **IF.. THEN** branch in the line, as if the condition is true then ORIC will jump to the new line and ignore any other statement in the original line.

An easier way to get pauses on ORIC is to use the WAIT command.

25 WAIT N will delay execution of the program for N lots of 10 milliseconds.

* * * * * * * * *

SUBROUTINES

At this stage you may be wondering about sections of a program that occur several times, but can't be achieved using simple **FOR/NEXT** loops.

For instance, in our counting program, you might want to tell people that the wait between numbers was intentional.

You send the program to a *subroutine*, where it waits, prints the message, then returns to the place where it left the main program.

```
10    FOR X = 1 TO 10
20    GOSUB 1000
30    PRINT X
40    NEXT
1000  PRINT "THIS IS A SHORT BREAK"
1010  WAIT 50
1020  RETURN
```

* * * * * * * * *

ON...GOTO

Sometimes, in the course of a program, it's useful to be able to branch to different parts of the program according to the results of

18

some calculation. This is easy using the **ON....GOTO** command. All you need to know are the expected results of the calculation and the relevant line numbers to branch to.

```
50    INPUT "CHOOSE 1,2 OR 3";X
60    ON X GOTO 100, 200, 300
70    PRINT "NUMBER NOT CHOSEN": STOP
100   PRINT "1 CHOSEN": STOP
200   PRINT "2 CHOSEN": STOP
300   PRINT "3 CHOSEN" : STOP
```

Line 50 expects an input. If **X** is 1, control branches to the first line number after **GOTO**, i.e. 100; if X is 2, it branches to the second line number, i.e. 200 and if it is 3, it branches to the third number, i.e. 300. If any other positive number is input, the program continues to the next statement following **ON....GOTO**

A similar command is **ON....GOSUB**, which will branch to a particular subroutine. When the program returns, it will continue from the next statement after the **ON....GOSUB**.

* * * * * * * * *

WHAT ELSE?

So far, we have only used **IF/THEN** in its simple form. It is possible to extend its power by using **ELSE**. Look at this:

```
10    FOR X = 1 TO 5
20    INPUT A
30    IF A > 10 THEN PRINT "TOO BIG" ELSE PRINT "O.K."
40    NEXT
```

If the condition is true then the first command is obeyed; if false, then the command following **ELSE**. If the program has not been told to branch, then execution will continue from the next program line.

* * * * * * * * *

REPEAT/UNTIL

If you wish to repeat a series of instructions a certain number of times, then it is easy to use a **FOR/NEXT** loop. This will be repeated the number of times that is set up in the first line, e.g.

FOR N = 1 TO 5

will loop five times. If you wish to loop until a certain condition is true, it is difficult to know what value to put in the loop counter.

REPEAT allows you to loop any number of times, and tests at the end of each loop to check if the conditon is met in the **UNTIL** line. This short program demonstrates this

```
10   REPEAT
20   D = D + INT(RND(1)*6) + 1
30   PRINT D
40   UNTIL D > 20
50   STOP
```

This simulates a situation where a die is being thrown, and will continue to be thrown until the total exceeds 20. It would not be possible to know the number of loops before the condition in line 40 is met, so a **FOR/NEXT** loop cannot be used. It would be possible to imitate this action using a **GOTO** statement **IF** the condition was not met, but the structure of the program would not be clear on reading the listing, so **REPEAT** should be used where possible.

Note that as with **FOR/NEXT**, the condition is tested at the end, so the loop is always negotiated at least once.

* * * * * * * * *

Before we go on to more interesting areas such as the pictures and sound, there is one last thing you can do to make your programs easier to read.

Use **REM** statements to explain lines. **REM** stands for remark and is ignored by ORIC. It is only there for your benefit when reading through the listing, or for when you show the program to others. This will show how you can use **REM**.

```
10   REM COPYRIGHT F. BLOGGS
20   FOR N = 1 TO 10 : REM COUNTS LOOP
30   PRINT "FRED IS MAGIC"
40   NEXT N
```

50 END
60 REM THIS IS A RATHER SILLY PROGRAM

Use **REM** statements to label your subroutines. Note that you can have have more than statement on a line, but each statement must be separated by a colon — See line 20.

1000 REM SUBROUTINE TO WAIT FOR A SHORT TIME
1010 WAIT 100
1020 RETURN

You can use ' instead of **REM**, but only as a comment at the end of a line.

10 PRINT ''HELLO'' 'THIS SAYS HELLO

is permissable.

10 ' COPYRIGHT ORIC LTD

is not permissable

Basic isn't hard to learn, and this is only a brief guide. You will become more proficient the more you use it.

* * * * * * *

I hear and I forget
I see and I remember
I do and I understand

Old Chinese proverb.

CHAPTER 4
Colour and Graphics

4.   Colour and Graphics

When you switch ORIC on it automatically goes into **TEXT** mode, i.e. you can use the screen to type on directly and when it's full, it will scroll up automatically. The **TEXT** area is also used for low-resolution graphics.

Before you experiment with **LORES,** it would be a good idea to discover which colours are available for use. There are two colour commands, **INK** and **PAPER**. These set the foreground and background colours, respectively, and can be used either as direct commands or in programs. They have to be followed by a number (Ø to 7) to specify which colour, and can be used in **TEXT** or **HIRES** modes.

    Ø   BLACK
    1   RED
    2   GREEN
    3   YELLOW
    4   BLUE
    5   MAGENTA
    6   CYAN
    7   WHITE

Try them out now. If you're used to computers that have to clear the screen before they can change colour, you will find that ORIC doesn't need to do this.

Here is a short program to show you all of ORIC's colour combinations.

```
 5   REM COLOURS
10   TEXT
20   FOR N = 1 TO 25
30   PRINT "THIS TEXT IS IN THE FOREGROUND
     COLOUR"
40   NEXT N
50   FOR I = Ø to 7
60   FOR P = Ø to 7
70   INK I : PAPER P
```

```
80   WAIT 100
90   NEXT P
100  NEXT I
210  INK 7 : PAPER 4
```

Of course, when the foreground and background colours are the same, you won't be able to read the words!

For low-resolution graphics, you can use the screen in **TEXT** mode or you can enter **LORES 0** or **LORES 1**. The screen area available for plotting is from 0 to 38 in the X axis (horizontal) and from 0 to 26 in the Y axis (vertical). Position 0,0 is at the top left hand corner of the screen. The far left column cannot be used, as it contains the attribute that controls the background or **PAPER** colour of that row.

The next column controls foreground or **INK** colour, but may be used in **TEXT** mode. If **LORES 0** or **LORES 1** are selected, the screen is cleared to background black, and the attribute for either standard or alternate character set is also placed on the far left of the screen.

LORES 0 uses the standard character set, and **LORES 1**, the alternate set.

Try this:

```
10   LORES 0
20   PLOT 16,12,"HELLO"
```

If you run this short program, **HELLO** will be printed in the centre of the screen. You could use the program in Chapter 9 to define other character's using the standard character set. The **PLOT** command would save you having to **POKE** into the screen memory.

If you now type

10   LORES 1

If line **20** is still intact, instead of **HELLO** appearing, a strange set of blocks will be printed. These are characters from the alternate set, and these particular ones are those that share the same ASCII codes as the letters in **HELLO**. This is the only difference between **LORES 0** and **LORES 1**.

This program will print out the complete set of alternate characters.

```
 5   REM ** ALTERNATE CHARACTERS **
10   FOR N = 32 TO 128
20   PRINT N,CHR$(27);"I";CHR$(N)
30   PRINT
40   WAIT 25
50   NEXT N
```

You can use this program to select characters to form your own graphics shapes. This is one way in which it can be used.

```
 1   REM *** MONSTER ***
 2   REM *** LORES 0/1 DEMO ***
 5   LORES 1
 6   D = 0
 9   REPEAT
10   A$ = "F9":B$ = "6I"
20   FOR C = 0 TO 35
30   PLOT C,D,A$
35   PLOT C,D + 1,B$
45   PLOT C,D," "
50   PLOT C,D + 1,"   "
55   NEXT C
56   SHOOT
60   D = D + 2
70   UNTIL D = 26
75   EXPLODE
80   CLS
```

The characters in **A$** and **B$** do not appear in their normal form, as **LORES 1** has been selected. The rest of the program sends the composite character along the rows successively until row 26 is reached, when it will explode!

To see the standard characters, simply type **LORES 0** in line 5. Should you need to mix alternate and standard characters on the same screen, i.e. to mix text and graphics, then it is easy. To use standard characters in **LORES 1** , **CHR$(8)** will switch to the standard set, and **CHR$(9)** will switch back.

If you use them in reverse, you can of course, print alternate characters in **LORES 0.** Here are two programs to demonstrate this effect. In all programs using **LORES 0** or **LORES 1**, it is a good idea to switch off the flashing cursor by typing **CTRL** and **Q** at the same time. Repeating this action will switch the cursor back on.

```
 5   REM ** TEXT IN LORES 1 **
10   LORES 1
20   A$ = CHR$(8) + "HELLO" + CHR$(9)
30   FOR N = 2 TO 24
40   PLOT N,N,"KKKK"
50   PLOT N,26-N,A$
60   NEXT N
70   WAIT 500
80   CLS
```

```
 5   REM ** ALT. CHARS IN LORES 0 **
10   LORES 0
20   A$ = CHR$(9) + "HELLO" + CHR$(8)
30   FOR N = 2 TO 24
40   PLOT N,N,"KKKK"
50   PLOT N,26-N,A$
60   NEXT N
70   WAIT 500
80   CLS
```

* * * * * * * * *

SCREEN POSITIONS

If you need to know which characters are at a particular position on the screen in either **TEXT** or **LORES** modes, use **SCRN(X,Y).**

Type **CLS** to clear the screen. The cursor should now be at the top left hand corner. Type

PLOT 10,20,"A"

A capital **A** will appear near the bottom of the screen.

Type

PRINT SCRN (10,20)

The number **65** will be returned, as this is the ASCII code for the letter A.

Here is a short program that **REPEAT**s a loop until a falling missile reaches a target. **SCRN(X,Y)** detects when the missile is one place away from the target (the Ascii code for + is 43 — see line 220), and the program finishes with an explosion. After you have **RUN** the program, change the mode in which it operates, by adding line **115 LORES 0** or **115 LORES 1**. This will show you the different effects you get according to the mode you have selected.

```
100    :REM ** USE OF SCRN(X,Y) **
110    :CLS:INK1:PAPER4
120    :FOR N = 20 TO 25
130    :     PLOT N,26," + "
140    :NEXT N
150    :REPEAT
160    :     A = INT(RND(1)*36 + 2)
170    :       FOR P  =  0 TO 24
180    :       PLOT A,P,"V"
190    :       WAIT 4
200    :       PLOT A,P," "
210    :       NEXT P
220    :UNTIL SCRN(A,P + 1) = 43
230    :EXPLODE
```

This program has been indented to make it easier to understand. It will work perfectly well with the initial colons and spaces removed. For a detailed explanation, consult Chapter 12.

To complete this section on low-resolution graphics, here is a program to show how background colours can be plotted in a circle.

```
10    REM **** LORES COLOUR PLOTTING ****
20    LORES 0
30    STP = 2*PI/50
40    R = 10:X = 10:Y = 10
50    REPEAT
60    E = 18 + RND(1)*6
```

27

```
70   PLOT X + R*SIN(C),Y + R*COS(C),E
80   C = C + STP
90   UNTIL C> 2*PI
100  REPEAT:UNTIL KEY$< > ""
110  CLS
```

* * * * * * * * *

HIGH RESOLUTION GRAPHICS

If you want to draw high resolution pictures, you need to type **HIRES**. Try it now.

You should find that the top of the screen goes black, leaving you just three lines for text at the bottom. This is useful, because you can type in drawing instructions, and see the effect on the screen above. In immediate mode, you can therefore use ORIC as a drawing tablet to try out your instructions. When they're correct, you can incorporate them in your programs.

If you want to get back into **TEXT** mode, just type **TEXT**, and the screen will go back to its original format. Both **TEXT** and **HIRES** can be used as commands within programs.

Before you start to draw anything, you have to imagine that the screen is divided up into 240 positions (labelled 0−239) across the screen, and 200 positions, (labelled 0−199) down the screen. Those across are called X positions, and those down Y positions. If you've used graphs, then you'll be familiar with this — the only difference is that the origin (0,0) is at the top left hand corner.

There are several specialist drawing commands that make graphics easy on ORIC.

We'll go through them one at a time so you can see their effect.

CURSET sets the cursor to an absolute **X,Y** position, or will plot that point. It must be followed by three parameters. (These are numbers that ORIC needs to know).

The **HIRES** cursor does not flash on the screen like the **TEXT** one.

i.e.:−

CURSET 120, 100, 1

will move the cursor to the centre of the screen and print a pixel, or small dot. The first parameter is how far across the screen (0−239), the second is how far down the screen (0−199) and the third is the **FB** number (FOREGROUND/BACKGROUND)

The **FB** codes are:—

   Ø   background colour
   1,   foreground colour
   2,   invert colours
   3,   null (do nothing)

Now type **HIRES** and experiment with **CURSET**.

The next graphics command is **CURMOV**. This is similar to **CURSET** except that **X & Y** are relative to the last position of the cursor. Again, ORIC needs to know **X, Y,** and **FB** numbers. Make sure that the value of **X** or **Y** plus the current cursor position does not take you off the screen, or you will get an error message.

DRAW X, Y, FB will draw a straight line from the current cursor position to the current cursor plus X and Y.

Try this short program. You should find it draws a square. Notice that negative numbers draw from right to left or from down to up. If the shape isn't quite "square" enough, try changing lines 3Ø and 5Ø.

```
 5   REM ** SQUARE **
10   HIRES
20   CURSET 6Ø, 4Ø, 3
30   DRAW 12Ø, Ø, 1
40   DRAW Ø, 12Ø, 1
50   DRAW - 12Ø, Ø, 1
60   DRAW Ø, - 12Ø, 1
```

REMEMBER:— Changing modes, or even typing **HIRES** again, will rub out your picture permanently!

                  * * * * * * * * *

PATTERNS

ORIC has yet another trick for you. When you switch on, the **DRAW** command is set to draw a continuous line. It's possible, however, to draw dotted lines, dashed lines, etc., according to your own specification.

This is how it works. If you remember it was mentioned earlier that ORIC thinks in 8 bit bytes, so you can count from Ø to 255 is using 8 zeros and ones. When ORIC is switched on, the number 255 is loaded into the pattern mask. (255 is written as 11111111 in binary code.)

You can set the mask to any number from 0 to 255 to get different effects. If you want equal sized dashes, you could type **PATTERN 15**.

15 is 00001111 in binary

i.e. $8 + 4 + 2 + 1$, so half the line is "on" and half is "off". Try drawing the square again, but this time reset the pattern mask to different numbers. There is nothing to stop you having two sides continuous, one dotted and one dashed. To help you understand how it works, just add this line as a starter.

15 PATTERN 170

(170 is 10101010 in binary).

It should send you dotty!

* * * * * * * * *

For a really exciting look at ORIC'S capabilities in **HIRES** mode, try this short program which generates interference patterns by drawing lines close to each other.

```
 5   REM ** MOIRE **
10   HIRES
20   FOR A = 0 TO 1
30   FOR B = 0 TO 239 STEP 6
40   CURSET 0, 199*A,3
50   DRAW B,199 - 398*A,1
60   CURSET 239,199*A,3
70   DRAW - B, 199 - 398*A,1
80   NEXT B: NEXT A
```

* * * * * * * * *

CHAR

If you were to try to **PRINT** in **HIRES** mode, you would only get text on the bottom 3 lines. There is a command however, that lets you print anywhere you like on the high resolution screen. Type **NEW** to clear the memory, then **HIRES**. Now set the cursor to the middle of the screen by typing **CURSET 120, 100, 3**. Now type **CHAR 65,0,1**. You should have a capital **A** in the middle of the screen.

CHAR is the command, and is followed by three parameters. **CHAR X, S, FB**.

X is the A.S.C.I.I. code (32 – 127)

S is either 0 (standard character set) or 1 (alternate set)

FB is foreground/background value (0-3)

A.S.C.I.I. (usually pronounced "Askey") stands for American Standard Code for Information Interchange. It is fairly standardized and assigns code numbers to letters, figures and symbols. (see appendix). There is a BASIC command ASC that returns the value of a character in a string, and this will save time as you will see in the next program.

```
 5  REM ** SIDEPRINT **
10  HIRES
20  CURSET 50, 50, 3
30  N$ = "HELLO I'M ORIC"
40  FOR A = 1 TO LEN (N$)
50  CHAR ASC (MID$(N$,A,1)),0,1
60  CURMOV 10,10,0
70  NEXT A
```

Lines 40 to 70 contain a loop that scans the length of N$ and prints the characters according to the **CURMOV** command.

Change **N$** to your name, or try changing the **CURMOV** parameters so you can see what happens. Be careful you don't go off the screen, or you will get an error message.

* * * * * * * * *

CIRCLES

To draw circles, simply type in **CIRCLE**, followed by two numbers — first the radius, then the **FB** code. The centre will be at the current cursor position. Be careful your radius does not take the circumference off the screen. Try this as a direct command in **HIRES** mode.

CURSET 120, 100, 3

then

CIRCLE 50,1

If you have previously set **PATTERN** to a different value, the circle will be drawn in dots, etc.

Try this program, for an interesting effect.

```
100  :REM ** LACE CIRCLES **
110  :HIRES
120  :CURSET 120,100,3
130  :FOR N = 99 TO 1 STEP −1
140  :  CIRCLE N,1
150  :  PATTERN 100 − N
160  :NEXT N
```
                    * * * * * * * * *

POINTS

If you want to know if any particular pixel on the screen is in fore-ground or background colour, e.g. if there is a space invader at the centre of the screen, then **POINT** is the command you need. To see how it works, try this in direct mode.

Type **HIRES**

Now type

CURSET 0,0,0 (cursor set at position 0,0 in background colour).
Now type

TEXT

next

PRINT POINT (0,0)

As 0,0 is set to background, you will get 0 printed. Type **HIRES**. This time type **CURSET 0,0,1** (cursor set at position 0,0 in foreground colour).
Now

TEXT,

then

PRINT POINT (0,0).

This time you should get −1, as the pixel is set to foreground.
                    * * * * * * * * *

FILL

This is a useful command that can fill an area of so many rows with a value and so many character cells with a value, between Ø and 127. There are 2ØØ rows, 4Ø cells per row. The value produces colours and patterns according to the attributes. (see appendix and chapter 7 for details).

Here is a short program to show you the fine detail that ORIC can achieve.

```
 5   HIRES
1Ø   FOR N = Ø to 199
2Ø   X = RND (1) * 8 + 16
3Ø   FILL 1, 1, X
4Ø   NEXT N
```

Line 2Ø chooses background colours at random from line Ø (top) to line 199 (bottom).

Experiment to find what the other attributes will achieve.

This program demonstrates mixing graphic patterns with colour and flashing attributes.

Note that line 13Ø avoids using the control codes that disturb the screen synchronization.

```
1ØØ   :REM **FILL DEMO **
11Ø   :HIRES
12Ø   :REPEAT
13Ø   :   A = RND(1)*128 + 1:IF A> 23 AND A< 32 THEN 13Ø
14Ø   :   CURSET RND(1)*9Ø + 1Ø,RND(1)*9Ø + 1Ø,1
15Ø   :   FILL RND(1)*9Ø + 1,1,A
16Ø   :UNTIL KEY$< > ""''
               * * * * * * * * *
```

DOUBLE HEIGHT AND FLASHING CHARACTERS

If you want special characters, e.g. flashing or in double height, there is a routine in ORIC that will achieve this for you.

If you look at the appendix for ORIC attributes, you will see a table specifying all the effects that are available. You will also need to refer to the table that covers *control characters*.

Control D toggles auto double height on/off. This can only be accessed through a print statement. Type **PRINT CHR$(4)**

Anything you enter now will appear twice in consecutive rows. Try it out. Help! How do we stop it?

As it's a toggle action switch, typing **PRINT CHR$(4)** a second time will turn this action off. The other control characters are achieved in a similar manner. But... back to the double flashers! The following program will give you the effect you desire.

    10   PRINT CHR$(12)
    20   PRINT CHR$(4); CHR$(27);"N DOUBLE FLASH CHARACTERS"
    30   PRINT CHR$(4)

Don't be alarmed if it looks fearsome; I'll explain each line at a time.

Line 10 clears the screen. It also ensures that you start at the top of the screen. You'll see why this is important when we add line 15 later.

Line 20 contains several statements. **CHR$(4)** switches on the auto double height (to save typing everything in twice), **CHR$(27)** is A.S.C.I.I. code for escape (to start the escape character routine) and the N in the quotes selects double height and flashing characters for the rest of the text — it won't be printed itself.

Line 30 toggles the auto D/H off.

Try changing the message in quotes, as well as altering the escape code, e.g. **"J HELLO"** will produce double height non-flashing characters.

When you've discovered how to achieve different effects, add this line: **15 PRINT** — then **RUN** the program. From the strange result, you will see how important it is to start on even line number (0,2,etc.)

In conclusion, here is a program that uses many of the high-resolution graphics commands. It also demonstrates how information for drawing commands can be held in **DATA** statements.

```
100   :REM ** PENNY FOR YOUR THOUGHTS**
110   :HIRES
120   :X = 100:Y = X
130   :CURSETX,Y,1
140   :PAPER6:INK1
150   :CIRCLE70,1      '**FRONT WHEEL**
160   :REPEAT
170   :  CURSETX,Y,3
180   :  DRAW69*SIN(F),69*COS(F),1
190   :  F = F + . 1
200   :UNTIL F> 2*PI
210   :F = 0
220   :CURSET 200,140,3
230   :CIRCLE30,1      '**BACK  WHEEL**
240   :REPEAT
250   :  DRAW29*SIN(F),29*COS(F),1
260   :  CURSET200,140,3
270   :  F = F + . 1
280   :UNTILF> 2*PI
290   :CURSET100,15,3
300   :REPEAT
310   :  READ A,B
320   :  DRAW A,B,1
330   :UNTIL B = 25
340   :CURSET 160,20,3
350   :FOR N = 1 TO 10 '**TEXT 1**
360   :  READ L
370   :  CHAR L,0,1
380   :  CURMOV 7,0,3
390   :NEXT
400   :CURSET 160,32,3
410   :FOR N = 1 TO 9 '**TEXT 2**
420   :  READ L
430   :  CHAR L,0,1
440   :  CURMOV 7,0,3
450   :NEXT
500   :DATA −10,0,10,10,0,20,0,−20,40,0
510   :DATA −10,−10,15,0,−5,10,60,60,0,25
520   :DATA 79,82,73,67,32,82,73,68,69,83
530   :DATA 84,79,32,87,79,82,75,33,33
```

CHAPTER 5
Editing Basic programs

5. Editing Basic programs

When you write a program and wish to change a line, there are several methods of altering or deleting existing instructions.

If the whole line is incorrect, then typing the line number followed by [**RETURN**] will delete the entire line.

    10 PRINT "HELLO"
    20 PRINT "OOPS!"
    30 PRINT "GOODBYE"

Type:—

    20 [RETURN]

Now type:—

LIST

You will see the program listing as before, but this time with line 20 missing

    10 PRINT "HELLO"
    30 PRINT "GOODBYE"

If you wish to delete all the lines in a program, then type **NEW**.

If you are typing a line in, and discover that you have made a mistake, you can rub out the last character entered by pressing the **DEL** key. Press **DEL** twice and the cursor will backspace (move to the left) two positions.

To delete a complete line as you are entering it, hold down **CTRL** and **X**. A backslash will appear at the end of the line, and the cursor will jump down to the start of a new line.

If you **LIST** a long program, you probably find that it flashes up the screen too fast to read. To halt the listing, press the space bar once. Pressing any key will continue the listing. To halt the listing completely, hold down **CTRL** and **C**. Control C will also stop the execution of most Basic programs. They can be restarted by typing **CONT** (for continue), unless you have changed any of the program or its variables. Then you will have to use **RUN** or **GOTO**.

* * * * * * * * *

COPYING

It would be very time-consuming to have to re-type whole lines, particularly if they contain complicated information. You are not allowed to have lines that are longer than 78 characters. Very long program lines are difficult to read and spoil the lay-out of the listings. ORIC will give out a **PING** if you try to exceed this number.

Should you need to change a line, ORIC has a **COPY** facility. To see it in action, type this short program in.

```
10   REM ** EDIT TEST **
20   A = 20:B = 30
30   C = A*B
40   PRINT C
```

If you decide that line 20 should read **A = 25: B = 5**, and that line 30 should read **C = A + B**, this is what you do. **LIST** the program and it will appear on the screen. It is a good idea to press control L (**CTRL** and **L** at the same time) to clear the screen each time before you **LIST** the program.

You can now move the cursor up the screen using the arrow keys next to the space bar. The cursor will move in the direction of the arrow on the key. When the cursor is next to line 20, hold down the **CTRL** key, and at the same time press **A**. The cursor will move to the right and each character it passes over will be entered in the input buffer (a temporary store).

When the cursor is over the **0** in 20, release **CTRL** and **A**, and press **5**. A **5** will appear instead of the **0**. Continue to copy the line using control A until the cursor is positioned over the 3 in 30. Release control A and enter **5**. The **5** will appear in place of the 3.

As you do not want the **0** in your new line, simply press [**RETURN**] and the edited line will be stored in the program memory. The screen display will show **A = 25: B = 50**, which may make you think it is incorrect. Clear the screen as before and **LIST** the program. Voila! — Line 20 now reads **A = 25: B = 5**.

Because you did not copy the **0** at the end of the line, it was not stored as part of the new line. To change line 30, move the cursor up to the line and then copy as far as * using control A. Enter + then copy **B** and press [**RETURN**].

Remember — moving the cursor anywhere on the screen does not alter the program lines. Program lines are entered by copying existing screen characters using control A, or by entering new ones from the keyboard. Control X will allow you to escape from the line, the cursor keys can jump over letters, **DEL** will delete mistakes and [**RETURN**] will enter the new line.

Until you are confident in using these features, always clear the screen and **LIST** the new line to ensure it has been entered as you wish. You will discover that you can edit and copy lines extremely quickly and you will soon become proficient at using the various editing facilities on ORIC.

* * * * * * * * *

TRON and TROFF

If you are developing a Basic program and, in spite of all your attempts, it does not work as expected, gives consistently strange results, or simply stops execution with an error message, then it is useful to know if the flow of control within the program is actually as you intended it. Oric has two commands that allow you to do this.

TRON turns on a trace facility that prints up the line number being executed. The line number itself is surrounded by brackets so that it is not mistaken for the actual screen display. **TRON** cannot be entered as a direct command but has to be inserted in a program complete with line number, e.g:—

```
50   TRON
```

Here is an example of a program that does not work! Type it in and **RUN** it.

```
10   FOR N = 1 TO 4
20   READ D
30   ON D GOSUB 100, 200, 300, 400
40   NEXT N
50   STOP
100  PRINT "I"
110  RETURN
200  PRINT "AM"
210  RETURN
300  PRINT "ORIC"
310  RETURN
```

```
400  PRINT "THAT'S WHO"
410  RETURN
500  DATA 1,2,3
```

You will see that there is something wrong with the **ON**...
GOSUB line when it is compared to the **DATA** line.

If you enter

```
5   TRON
```

then **RUN** the program, the screen will fill with line numbers. You
can see that they never reach **400**, and a check at the **DATA** line
will reveal why — it is missing a figure 4.

If you only wished to examine say, the working of a subroutine, it
would be possible to start the subroutine with **TRON** (**TR**ace **ON**)
and finish it with **TROFF** (**TR**ace **OFF**).

CHAPTER 6
Number crunching

6. Number crunching

As you have already discovered, ORIC can handle very large numbers and also very small ones, both positive and negative. The larger numbers grow, the more figures they require, so 10 needs two figures, 100 needs three, and so on. This can become untidy and difficult to read and write when the number gets very large. There is a way of writing numbers that is a lot more compact, called scientific or exponent notation.

$$10 \text{ can be written } 1 \times 10^1 \text{ (10)}$$
$$100 \text{ can be written } 1 \times 10^2 \text{ (10 x 10)}$$
$$1000 \text{ can be written } 1 \times 10^3 \text{ (10 x 10 x 10)}$$
and so on

ORIC could write 1×10^3 as $1.00000000E + 3$. In fact, numbers up to 999999999 are usually shown as they are normally written, as ORIC is accurate to 9 digits.

Try these:-

PRINT 999999999 * 1

then
PRINT 9999999999 * 1

This shows you how scientific notation works, and also how the number is rounded off.

Enter large numbers and see how Oric prints them. You can also enter numbers such as $2.3E + 4$ to see what their equivalent is. An easy way to remember how to convert these numbers is to say $2.3E + 4$ means
"Write down 2.3 Move the figures 4 places to the left. Fill any spaces with zeros".

    2.3
   23.0 ← 1 place (or times 10)
  230.0 ← 2 places (or times 100)
 2300.0 ← 3 places (or times 1000)
23000.0 ← 4 places (or times 10000)

So 2.3E + 4 is the same as 23000

2.3E – 4 What does this mean? The negative sign after the E does not mean the number is negative, simply very small. It means:—
"Write down 2.3 Move the figures 4 places to the right. Fill any spaces with zeros".

2.3

0.23   → 1 place (or divide by 10)

0.023   → 2 places (or divde by 100)

0.0023 → 3 places (or divide by 1000)

0.00023 → 4 places (or divide by 10000)

So 2.3E – 4 is a very small number: 0.00023. If the number is a large negative number it would be written – 2.3E + 4. If the number is a very small negative number, it would be written – 2.3E – 4 Make sure you understand these differences if you wish to understand how ORIC handles numbers.

* * * * * * * * *

INT

INT is a function that returns the largest whole number less than or equal to the value in brackets. Try these to see if Oric returns the answers you expect:—

PRINT INT (1.5)

PRINT INT (2)

PRINT INT (– 2)

PRINT INT (– 1.5)

Note particularly the result of the last example — **INT** always rounds to a number less than that in brackets, unless it is already an integer.

* * * * * * * * *

ABS

ABS returns the absolute value of a number. If it is positive, it remains so. If it is negative, it becomes positive.

Try these:—

PRINT ABS (4.3)

PRINT ABS (– 4.3)

* * * * * * * * *

SGN

SGN returns either – 1, Ø or 1, according to whether the value in the brackets is negative, zero or positive. Try this to see how it works:-

```
10  FOR N = -5 TO 5
20  PRINT N, SGN(N)
30  NEXT N
```

* * * * * * * * *

DATA

If you have a lot of numbers that will be used in a program then it is possible to have them stored in the program as **DATA**, rather than have to type them in each time. This short example shows how to incorporate this information in your programs:-

```
10  FOR N = 1 TO 5
20  READ A
30  S = S + A
40  NEXT N
50  PRINT "SUM = " S
60  DATA 1,3,8,6,4
```

Line 20 **READ**s the **DATA**, one item at a time, and assigns that value to the variable **A**. It is added to **S** (initially zero) each time and printed out at line 50.

When the program is **RUN**, a pointer moves along each item as it is **READ**, and it remains at the last item it reaches. If you type in **GOTO 10**, the pointer is not reset, and you will get an **OUT OF DATA** error message. **RESTORE** is a command that resets the pointer in a program. Add **15 RESTORE** and see the effect this has on the program. The pointer is reset to the first **DATA** item each time the loop is executed, so 1 is added to **S** each time, and the rest of the **DATA** is ignored.

* * * * * * * * *

ARRAYS

Sometimes it is a better idea to collect similar variables together, instead of giving them different names. Arrays have brackets following the variable letter so you can identify an element. e.g. $N(1), N(2), N(3)$ and $N(4)$ are all elements in the array **N**.

Oric reserves space for up to 10 elements in an array, automatically. If you require more room, you will have to use the **DIM** statement. e.g. **DIM N(14)** will reserve space for 15 elements. (Arrays start with zero, not one, in most forms of Basic).

One reason for using arrays rather than simple variables is that they can fit in **FOR/NEXT** loops easily.

```
10   FOR N = 1 TO 5
20   A(N) = N*N
30   NEXT N
40   FOR X = 1 TO 5
50   PRINT X, A(X)
60   NEXT X
```

Lines 10 to 30 load the array **A(N)** with the squares of the loop number (**N**). Lines 40 to 60 print the contents of the array on the screen. Note that it is not necessary to fill every element in an array. Any "empty" elements will contain zero.

An array like those we have just considered is similar to a column of numbers, but it is also possible to have rows and columns — in other words, a two-dimensional array. Multi- dimensional arrays must be dimensioned before use.

```
10   DIM A(5,5)
20   FOR N = 1 TO 5
30   FOR M = 1 TO 5
40   A(N,M) = N*M
50   NEXT M,N
```

This will load numbers into 25 locations. You can probably see from the program that they happen to be the answers to some simple multiplication sums.

			N			
	0	1	2	3	4	5
0	0	0	0	0	0	0
1	0	1	2	3	4	5
M 2	0	2	4	6	8	10
3	0	3	6	9	12	15
4	0	4	8	12	16	20
5	0	5	10	15	20	25

Contents of array A(N,M) after execution of program.

The numbers in the brackets identify which element you wish to refer to, and are known as subscripts. e.g. **A(2,3)** is 6 and **A(5,5)** is 25.

If you wish to have even more dimensions, than it is perfectly possible. It is important to remember, however, that even **DIM N(10,10,10)** has **1000** elements, and you may run out of memory rather quickly!

* * * * * * * * *

LOGS

I have mentioned that numbers can be written using scientific notation. e.g. $1.6E + 2$ is the same as 160. More usually $1.6E + 2$ would be written 1.6×10^2 which means $1.6 \times 10 \times 10$ or 1.6×100. The small 2 in 10^2 means "write the large number down this number of times and multiply them together". e.g. 10×10.

So 10^4 means $10 \times 10 \times 10 \times 10$ or 10000. The small number is called the index or exponent. 10^4 is usually read as "10 raised to the power of 4" or just "10 to the power of 4".

This gives us an introduction to logarithms, or logs for short, because the log of a number is the power to which 10 must be raised to produce that number. i.e. 4 is the log of 10,000.

To find the log of a number between 1 and 10, we have to find the index that will produce that number. It must be between $0 + 1$. If you type

PRINT LOG (5)

then the log will be returned. You should get

0.698970004.

To check if this really is the log of 5, try raising 10 to that power and see if 5 is produced.
Type

PRINT 10 ⌐ 0.698970004.

and see if you were right. (The sign ⌐ means "to the power of" and is SHIFT 6 on the keyboard). Remember $10^{\log x} = X$.

As well as base 10 or common logs, there are also natural logs available on Oric. Type

PRINT LN(5)

You should get

1.60943791

which is the natural log of 5. How can there be more than one log? Base 10 logs are the power to which 10 must be raised to produce that number. Natural logs are the power to which e must be raised to produce that number. e is

2.718281828

e is the result of this series

$$e = 1 + 1 + \frac{1}{2} + \frac{1}{2 \times 3} + \frac{1}{2 \times 3 \times 4} \ldots \ldots \text{ etc.}$$

The natural exponential of a number is the inverse of the natural log and can be produced by typing PRINT EXP (X)

Therefore X = EXP (LN(X))

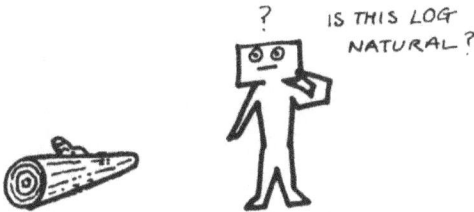

To find the logarithm of a number to another base, use the formula

LOG base z (X) = LOG_e (X)/LOG_e (Z)

Log e is of course the same as LN on Oric.

* * * * * * * * *

NUMBER BASES

So far we have encountered binary numbers and decimal numbers. Perhaps you are confused by so many different ways of representing the same quantities. In fact, they are not really as difficult to grasp as they may appear — it all comes down to how we choose to group numbers. Normally, we group things in tens — probably

47

because we have ten fingers and thumbs — there is no other likely reason. Our whole counting system uses groups of ten. When we have ten groups of ten, it forms a hundred, and ten hundreds form a thousand and so on.

e.g. 3742 is made up of 3 thousands, 7 hundreds, 4 tens and 2 units. The largest figure you may have in any column is 9. One more, and you have enough for one group of 10 in the next column.

e.g. 9
      + 1
      ───
      10
      ───

Just suppose that humans had 8 fingers and thumbs. They would have used these symbols: 0,1,2,3,4,5,6,7. 8 and 9 would not exist.

e.g. 7
      + 1
      ───
      10
      ───

The largest figure you may now have in any column is 7. One more makes a group of eight, so the answer is 10. This is not read as "ten" but "one-zero" in "base eight". To show that it is not a normal (or decimal or denary or base 10) number, then it is usual to write it 10_8.

Just as the column headings in base 10 numbers are in tens,

e.g. | thousands | hundreds | tens | units |
|---|---|---|---|
| (10x10x10) | (10x10) | (10) | |

so in base eight, the headings are in eights,

e.g. | 512 | 64 | 8 | units |
|---|---|---|---|
| (8x8x8) | (8x8) | (8) | |

so 1241_8 is the same as
(1x512) + (2x64) + (4x8) + 1 = 673 in base 10.

In the language of the computer, binary or base 2, the same rules apply — but now there are only 2 digits, 0 + 1 and the groupings are in twos.

e.g.   16   8   4   2   units
      (2x2x2x2)   (2x2x2)   (2x2)   (2)

So in binary, the number 10111 is the same as

$(1 \times 16) + (0 \times 8) + (1 \times 4) + (1 \times 2) + 1 = 23$ in base 10.

This can get rather cumbersome when large numbers are involved. In face, you need 8 digits to make 255, and 65535 is 1111111111111111 — sixteen digits!

It would be possible to ignore binary code for large numbers and stick to base 10, but that would give no clue as to how the number was stored on a computer.

A compromise is reached by using base sixteen (or hexadecimal or hex as it is more usually called.) Base 16 needs 16 digits, so letters are used above 9. This means that counting in hexadecimal results in this:-

0,1,2,3,4,5,6,7,8,9,A,B,C,D,E,F

You can see that fifteen in hex is F, and so sixteen is 10. This gives column headings as follows:—

        4096   256   16   units
    $(16 \times 16 \times 16)$ (16×16) (16)

So 12AF in hex, is the same as
    $(1 \times 4096) + (2 \times 256) + (10 \times 16) + 15 = 4783$ in base 10.

Why choose such a horrifying number system? Perhaps you've guessed — it shows at a glance how the numbers are stored in a computer, by taking blocks of four bits at a time.

F0 can be stored in one byte

            F   0
        ‿‿‿   ‿‿‿
        1111   0000

The enormous binary number that is the equivalent of 65535 in base 10 becomes FFFF in hex. You may be able to see now why 65535 is the highest memory location you can address using two bytes.

Oric will recognize hexadecimal numbers as such, provided they are preceded by a #, pronounced "hash". So **PRINT #1A** produces **26**. Try out some conversions for yourself. The largest number you may convert is **#FFFF**. Check your results against the table in the appendices.

NOTE: You may find some books that identify hex numbers by use of a $, but Oric will interpret this as a string sign.

If you need to convert between hexadecimal and base 10 numbers, you would use #. i.e.

PRINT #10

will produce 16.

To convert a decimal or base ten number into a string containing the value and preceded by a #, type

PRINT HEX$(16)

This will produce #10. As with #, there is an upper limit of 65535 i.e. **#FFFF**. This program will print out base 10 numbers up to 255 and also their hexadecimal equivalent.

```
10   FOR N = 0 TO 255
20   PRINT N, HEX$(N)
30   NEXT N
```
* * * * * * * * *

MATHS ROUTINES

Although it is important not to think of computers purely as manipulators of numbers, there is no doubt that they make many maths tasks that are usually boring and repetitive, comparatively simple. Oric has many built in routines that assist "number-crunching".

If you needed to know all the square roots from 1 to 100, you would have to spend a long time looking in tables or pressing calculator keys. Oric can achieve this much more simply. Type in this program:—

```
10   CLS
20   FOR N = 1 TO 100
30   PRINT N, SQR(N)
40   NEXT N
```

If you **RUN** it, the numbers from 1 to 100 will flash down the left side of the screen, with their square roots next to them in the centre of the screen. Oric calculates them so fast that you probably found it difficult to read. Put in

35 WAIT 10

to slow the program down.

Oric can even calculate roots without using the SQR facility. There is a method of finding roots called the Newton-Raphson iterative method. Iteration means to keep on doing the same thing again and again — an ideal use for a loop on Oric. Each time, the guess is refined and gets closer to the correct answer. This short program shows the guesses, and stops when the answer is correct. (Line 80 jumps out of the loop if the guess is within ± 0.000001 of the right answer — just in case there is not an exact answer).

```
 5   REM *** ITERATIVE ROOTS ***
10   INPUT "THINK OF A NUMBER";S
20   INPUT "GUESS THE ROOT";G
30   PRINTG
40   X = S/G
50   G = (X + G)/2
60   R = G*G
70   IF R< (S + 0.000001) AND R>
     (S − 0.000001) THEN GOTO 90
80   GOTO 30
90   PRINT"ROOT = ";G
```

There is another use for ORIC's high-speed maths brain. The 17th Century mathematics Leibnitz, who made calculus possible, discovered a way of calculating π.

π is an irrational number; in other words, it can never be calculated to a finite number of decimal places.

Leibnitz discovered that this sequence approached closer and closer to the true value.

$$\pi \simeq 4(1 - \tfrac{1}{3} + \tfrac{1}{5} - \tfrac{1}{7} + \tfrac{1}{9} \ldots) \text{ etc.}$$

You should be able to see a regular pattern in the fractions. ORIC loves patterns, as they can be put in loops. If you were to try to calculate the above formula with pencil and paper it would take you a long time, even up to $-1/9$. — all the worse when you realize that the answer isn't close enough until you've looped several hundred times. Poor Leibnitz, but lucky you! Try this program.

```
 5   REM *** SLOW PI ***
10   CLS
20   DEF FNA(N) = ( - 1/N + 1/(N + 2))
30   FOR X = 3 TO 10003 STEP 4
40   S = S + FNA(X)
50   APPROX = 4*(1 + S)
60   PRINT APPROX
70   NEXT X
```

Line 20 defines a function, **A**, containing a variable **N**. This saves having a cumbersome line later. **FNA** actually calculates the series and is called at line 30. The loop goes up in steps of 4, starting with 3, so X is 3,7,11,15 etc. This makes correct increments and the result is printed at line 50. If you **RUN** the program, Oric will print a result for π that gets closer and closer to the actual result. Compare it with 3.1416 and you will see that it's not the fastest way to calculate π, even with ORIC.

To find π rather more quickly, simply type

PRINT PI

This will give you an accurate value of π to several places of decimals, as **PI** is stored as a constant by ORIC.

Remember that this means you cannot choose **PI** as a variable name, or indeed any word beginning with **PI**, such as **PIG = 8** or **PIPES = 78**, because **PI** is a reserved word.

* * * * * * * * *

RANDOM NUMBERS

There is a useful function on ORIC that is often used in games programs. This is **RND**, which will return a pseudo-random number. Due to the way computers generate random numbers, this will not be truly random, and it would be possible to discover a pattern in the series of numbers produced. This is not likely to be obvious unless you perform a statistical analysis on the series, so **RND** can for all normal purposes be considered truly random.

If you aren't sure what random num bers are, then consider a die. It has an equal chance of producing any numbers from 1 to 6. The order in which the numbers are actually produced in a series of throws is random. To simulate this on ORIC, try this program.

```
5   REM *** DICE THROWER ***
10  FOR N = 1 TO 10
20  PRINT"PRESS ANY KEY TO THROW DIE"
30  GET A$
40  A = INT(RND(1)*6) + 1
50  PRINT A
60  NEXT
```

Line 20 waits for any key to be pressed. Line 30 chooses a random number between $0 + 1$, multiplies it by 6, the **INT** function loses any decimal fraction, and finally, 1 is added. This ensures that a number from 1 to 6 will be produced.

RND(n) will produce a random number greater than or equal to 0 and less than 1, if **n** is a positive number. If **n** is a negative number, then the random seed is set to a particular number, and subsequent positive **n**'s will always produce the same sequence. If **n** is zero, the last random number generated will be produced.

* * * * * * * * *

To conclude this chapter, here is a program that utilizes many of the functions mentioned in this chapter. It also uses some string handling routines that you may not fully understand until you have read the relevant chapter. If necessary come back to it later.

Calendars are difficult to construct due to the awkwardness of the earth in not taking an exact number of days to pass round the sun. In fact, it takes 365.242216 days to make an exact year.

Various people, from Numa Pomilius and Julius Caesar down to Pope Gregory, have attempted to correct the calendar, but it is still not perfect.

All this makes it rather more complicated to calculate which day of the week a particular date fell on. The German mathematician, Gauss, worked out a formula that works for any date from 1752, when the Gregorian calendar was initiated in the U.K. and the American colonies.

```
5    REM *** DAY CALCULATOR ***
10   CLS
20   PRINT"ENTER DATE, MONTH & YEAR"
30   INPUT "DATE";D
40   IF D< 1 OR D> 31 THEN 30
50   INPUT "MONTH";M
60   IF M< 1 OR M> 12 THEN 50
70   INPUT "YEAR";Y
80   IF Y< 1752 OR Y > 8000 THEN 70
90   M = M - 2:IFM< 1 THEN M = M + 12:Y = Y - 1
100  Y$ = STR$(Y)
110  C = INT(Y/100)
120  Y = VAL(RIGHT$(Y$,2))
130  A = INT(2.6*M - 0.19) + D + Y + INT(Y/4) + INT
     (C/4) - C*2
140  DAY = INT((A/7 - INT(A/7))*7 + 0.1)
150  DAY = DAY + 1
160  FOR N = 1 TO DAY
170  READ DAY$
180  NEXT N
190  PRINT DAY$
200  DATA SUNDAY,MONDAY,TUESDAY,
     WEDNESDAY,THURSDAY,FRIDAY,SATURDAY
```

CHAPTER 7
More mathematical functions

7. More mathematical functions

TRIGONOMETRY

ORIC has many functions that you will recognize if you have a scientific calculator or if you remember your geometry lessons at school. These are SIN (sines) COS (cosines), TAN (tangents). They are ratios of lengths of sides of triangles for difference angles.

SHOULDN'T TRIANGLES BE IN THE MUSIC SECTION ?

ABC is a right-angled triangle. x is the angle at corner ACB. The side AB is opposite angle x, BC is adjacent to angle x, and AC is called the hypotenuse.

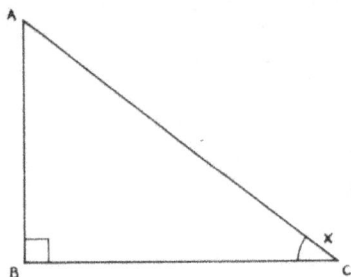

$$\frac{AB}{BC} = \frac{opposite}{adjacent} = \text{tangent of angle x}$$

$$\frac{AB}{AC} = \frac{opposite}{hypotenuse} = \text{sine of angle x}$$

$$\frac{BC}{AC} = \frac{adjacent}{hypotenuse} = \text{cosine of angle x}$$

You can probably see how the ratios change in these three example triangles:—

1.) When x is large

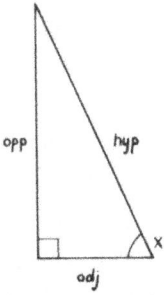

$$\text{TAN}(x) = \frac{\text{opp}}{\text{adj}} \rightarrow \quad \text{a large number that tends towards infinity as } x \text{ approaches } 90°$$

$$\text{SIN}(x) = \frac{\text{opp}}{\text{hyp}} \rightarrow \quad \text{tends towards 1 as } x \text{ approaches } 90°$$

$$\text{COS}(x) = \frac{\text{adj}}{\text{hyp}} \rightarrow \quad \text{tends towards } \emptyset \text{ as } x \text{ approaches } 90°$$

2.) When x is 45°

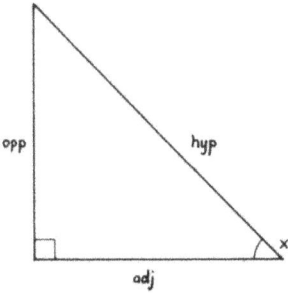

$$\text{TAN}(x) = \frac{\text{opp}}{\text{adj}} \rightarrow \quad 1$$

$$\text{SIN}(x) = \frac{\text{opp}}{\text{hyp}} \rightarrow \quad \frac{1}{\sqrt{2}}$$

$$\text{COS}(x) = \frac{\text{adj}}{\text{hyp}} \rightarrow \quad \frac{1}{\sqrt{2}}$$

3.) When x is small

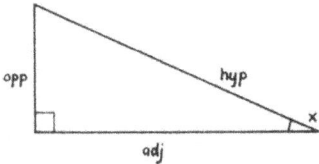

$$\text{TAN}(x) = \frac{\text{opp}}{\text{adj}} \rightarrow \quad \text{a small number that tends towards } \emptyset \text{ as } x \text{ approaches } 0°$$

$$\text{SIN}(x) = \frac{\text{opp}}{\text{hyp}} \rightarrow \quad \text{tends towards } \emptyset \text{ as } x \text{ approaches } 0°$$

$$\text{COS}(x) = \frac{\text{adj}}{\text{hyp}} \rightarrow \quad \text{tends towards 1 as } x \text{ approaches } 0°$$

You can obtain TAN, SIN & COS by simply typing **PRINT TAN (x)**, etc. The ony problem is that Oric, like most computers likes angles in radians, not degrees. Luckily degrees can be turned into radians, and vice versa very easily.

A quick recap on circles.

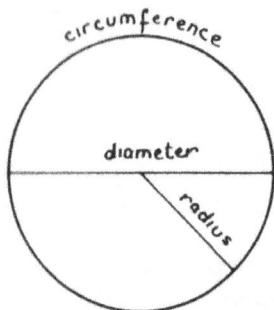

diameter = 2 x radius

$\pi = \dfrac{\text{circumference}}{\text{diameter}}$

$\pi = \dfrac{\text{circumference}}{2 \times \text{radius}}$

$\therefore$ circumference = 2 x π x radius

and radius $= \dfrac{\text{circumference}}{2 \times \pi}$

How many times would the radius fit round the circumference? More than 6 times — in fact 2 x π times. If you were to cut out a slice from the circle, so that the curved part equals the radius, r, then the angle at the centre, x, is 1 radian. One complete circle = 360° so 1 radian = $\dfrac{360°}{2\pi}$ = 57·29578°

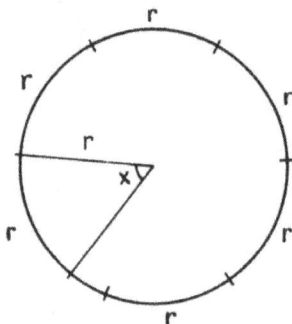

To convert radians to degrees, use the formula:—

degrees = $\dfrac{\text{radians x } 360}{2\pi}$ $\simeq$ radians x 57·29578

To convert degrees to radians, use the formula:—

radians = $\dfrac{2 \times \pi \times \text{degrees}}{360°}$ $\simeq$ $\dfrac{\text{degrees}}{57·29578}$

Here are some programs to show how ORIC can use trigonometric functions to draw on the screen, as well as calculate for you.

PROG. 1. Sine waves

```
 5   REM *** SINE ***
10   HIRES
20   DRAW 0,199,1
30   CURSET 0,100,3:DRAW 239,0,1
40   FOR A = - PI TO PI STEP 0.02
50   CURSET A*38 + 120,SIN(A)*99 + 99,1
60   NEXT
70   PRINT "SINE CURVE"
80   GET A$
```

This draws a sine curve from $-\pi$ to π. Line 70 prints on the 3 line text screen and holds it until any key is pressed at line 80. Change SIN in line 50 to COS and see the difference while ORIC plots a COSINE curve.

PROG. 2. Tower

```
  5   REM *** TOWER ***
 10   HIRES
 20   CURSET 20,20,3
 30   DRAW 0,160,1
 40   DRAW 200,0,1
 50   DRAW - 200, - 160,1
 60   CURSET 25,170,3
 70   A$ = "↑ TOWER"
 80   FOR N = 1 TO 6
 90   CHAR ASC(MID$(A$,N,1)),0,1
100   CURMOV 8,0,3
110   NEXT
120   CURSET 200,170,3
130   CHAR ASC("X"),0,1
140   INPUT "DISTANCE";D
150   INPUT "ANGLE X (DEGREES)";X
160   XR = X/57·29578
170   H = TAN(XR)*D
180   PRINT H;
```

This calculates the height of a tower, if you can supply the distance and the angle from your position to the top of the tower. Lines 30 to

50 draw the triangle, lines 70 to 110 are necessary to print on the high resolution screen, and line 160 converts degrees to radians, Note the semi-colon in line 180. This keeps the answer in view on the text window.

There is a list of derived functions in the Appendices. You can define these using **DEF FN**, or by use of the defined **&** character (see the Machine Code chapter) as an extension function.

CHAPTER 8
Words

8. Words

Earlier, we discovered that computers can manipulate any collection of symbols, not just numbers. So that ORIC knows that the symbols must be considered as such, and does not mistake them for variables, they have to be enclosed within quotes.

So,

PRINT A

will result in a zero being printed, as it is considered to be a variable.

PRINT "A"

will result in **A** being printed, as it is enclosed within quotes.

String variables are identified by a dollar sign at the end. e.g. **A$** or **A3$**. Remember that ORIC only reads the first two characters of a variable name, so **BIG$** is the same as **BIKE$**.

I ALWAYS THOUGHT STRING HANDLING MEANT LEARNING THE CATS CRADLE !

Strings are assigned using **LET**, although this is optional.

LET A$ = "HELLO"

is the same as

A$ = "HELLO".

The only simple mathematical operator that may be used with strings is + . So,

```
10   A$ = "HELLO"
20   B$ = A$ + A$
30   PRINT B$
```

will print **HELLOHELLO**.

Line 20 could not be written as **B$ = 2*A$**. Total length of a string must not exceed 255 characters.

To find the length of a string there is a function called **LEN**.

IF **A$ = "HELLO" THEN PRINT LEN (A$)**

will print **5**. This value can be assigned to a variable.

```
10   INPUT A$
20   L = LEN(A$)
30   PRINT A$ "CONTAINS";L;"CHARACTERS"
```

Although a string cannot be used as a number directly, it is possible to convert it into a number, using the **VAL** function.

```
10   A$ = "56"
20   V = VAL(A$)
30   PRINT V
```

Because **V** is not a string variable, it can be manipulated as a number, and **PRINT 2*V** will return a value of 112. If the first character in the string is an alphabetic character then a value of zero is returned.

```
10   A$ = "ORIC"
20   V = VAL(A$)
30   PRINT V
```

There is a function that works in the opposite direction. **STR$** converts a numeric expression into a string.

```
10   A = 128
20   A$ = STR$(A)
30   PRINT A$
```

You cannot tell the difference between **PRINT A** and **PRINT A$** — the results appear the same. However, **PRINT A + A** will produce **256**, whereas **PRINT A$ + A$** will produce **128 128** as ORIC treats them differently.

If you look at the end of this book, you will find a table entitled ASCII codes. These are also mentioned in Chapter 4.

Using the function **ASC** will return the code for any keyboard character. The function **CHR$** works in the reverse direction, and con-
verts a number between 32 and 128 into the corresponding character.
To list them all, run this program.

```
10   FOR N = 32 TO 128
20   PRINT "ASCII CODE" N "STANDS FOR" CHR$(N)
30   WAIT 20
40   NEXT N
```

Because all the characters have **ASCII** codes, they can be sorted
into order. As you can see, numerical order is the same as alphabetical order, so **Z**, which has the value **90**, is greater than **A** which has
the value **65**.

You can use the greater than (>) and the less than (<) signs to
compare strings, as well as numbers. Care must be taken, however,
to avoid mixing upper and lower case, and all lower case letters have
greater values than upper case, so although "**apple**" is less than
"**zebra**", "**apple**" is greater than "**Zebra**".

To assist you in manipulating strings, there are 3 more very useful
functions — **RIGHT$**, **LEFT$** and **MID$**. **RIGHT$** returns the
right hand portion of a string as follows:

A$ = "ABCDEFGHIJ"

PRINT RIGHT$ (A$,2)

will print "**IJ**". The number 2 is the quantity of characters to be
returned.

LEFT$ returns the left hand proportion of a string as follows:

A$ = "ABCDEFGHIJ"

PRINT LEFT$(A$,2)

will print "**AB**"

MID$ needs just a little more information.

A$ = "ABCDEFGHIJ"
PRINT MID$(A$,5,2)

will print "**EF**". The example means — return the 2 characters from
string **A$**, starting at position 5. The second number can be omitted,

in which case all the characters to the right of, and including, the first number are returned.

A$ = "ABCDEFGHIJ"
PRINT MID$(A$,5)

will print **"EFGHIJ"**.

Here is a short program that demonstrates these functions.

```
10   PRINT "ENTER A STRING"
20   INPUT A$
30   IF LEN(A$)< 3 THEN PRINT "TOO SHORT": GOTO
     10
40   PRINT A$ "IS";LEN(A$);"CHARACTERS LONG"
50   PRINT "IT STARTS WITH";LEFT$(A$,1)
60   PRINT "AND ENDS WITH";RIGHT$(A$,1)
70   PRINT "AND  HAS";MID$(A$,2,LEN(A$) – 2);  "IN
     THE MIDDLE"
```

Often it is easier to have information stored in a program. Just as it is possible to hold numbers in **DATA** statements, strings can be held just in a similar manner.

```
10   FOR X = 0 TO 3
20   READ NAME$(X)
30   PRINT NAME$(X)
40   NEXT
50   DATA TOM, TERESA, DENIS, MARTIN
```

The **DATA** is **READ** one name at a time and stored in array, **NAME$**. **NAME$(0)** is then **TOM**, **NAME$(1)** is **TERESA**, **NAME$(2)** is **DENIS**, and **NAME$(3)** is **MARTIN**.

String arrays are similar to numerical arrays. ORIC reserves space automatically for up to 11 elements (numbered 0 to 10). If you want more, then you must put in a **DIM** statement for the number you need e.g. **DIM A$ (19)** would create space for 20 elements.

There is one special thing to note about strings held in **DATA** lines. If you insert leading spaces, they will be ignored by ORIC. e.g.

DATA AB, C,DE

will lose the space before the **C**. If you want the space included, you must surround the whole item by quotes. e.g.

DATA AB," C",DE

When you **RUN** a program, the **DATA** pointer goes to the first item in the first **DATA** line and **READS** from there. If you **RUN** the name program, the data pointer will **READ** 4 items, then stay at the end. If you then enter

GOTO 10

the pointer cannot find any more items, so the error message

OUT OF DATA IN 20

appears. To send the pointer back in a program, use the command **RESTORE**. If you add this line to the program, you will find that you can use **GOTO 10** without getting an error message.

   35   RESTORE

Because it is in the loop, the pointer will be reset each time, and **TOM** will be loaded into all the elements of the array.
* * * * * * * * *

SORTING

To complete this chapter, here is a program that demonstrates some of the string handling techniques of ORIC, particularly the use of string arrays and string comparison.

There are many kinds of sorting methods that computers can use. All operate on the principle that words starting with letters that have low **ASCII** codes will finish the routine at the beginning of an array, those with high **ASCII** codes at the end, and the rest arranged in numerical and therefore alphabetical order in between.

This sample program loads the words to be sorted into an array **A$**, and uses **U$** as a temporary store while the list is worked through. **A$** is shuffled until the words are correctly ordered, when they are printed out in lines 150 to 170.

You could use this program as a sorting subroutine in your own programs and renumber it from, say, 2000.

```
5    REM ***SORT***
10   INPUT "NO. OF WORDS";N
15   DIM A$(N + 1)
20   FOR X = 0 TO N - 1
30   INPUT A$(X)
40   NEXT
50   FOR X = 0 TO N - 1
60   PRINT A$(X):NEXT
70   FOR K = 0 TO N - 1
80   FOR L = K + 1 TO N
90   IF A$(L)> = A$(K) THEN 130
100  U$ = A$(L)
110  A$(L) = A$(K)
120  A$(K) = U$
130  NEXT L
140  NEXT K
150  FOR X = 0 TO N
160  PRINT A$(X)
170  NEXT
```

CHAPTER 9
Advanced Graphics

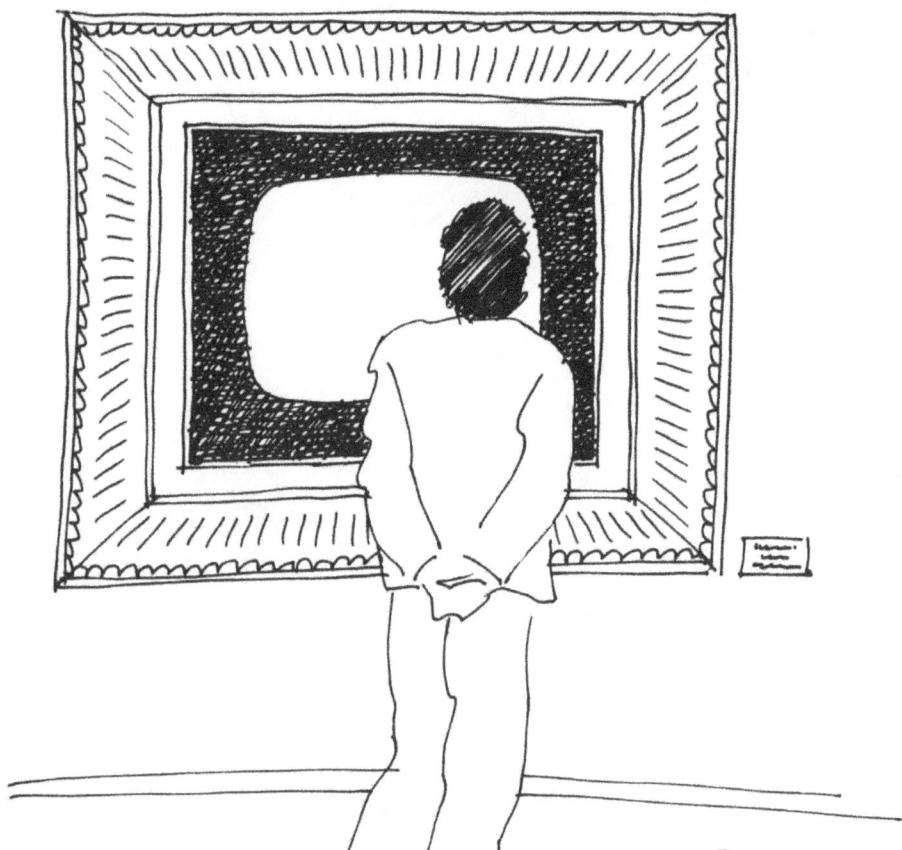

9. Advanced graphics

USER DEFINED GRAPHICS

When ORIC is switched on, both the standard and alternate character sets are loaded into Ram. The standard character set contains all the usual ASCII characters as shown in the appendix and the alternate character set contains teletext graphics. Either set can be completely or partly overwritten.

In a game, you may wish to use text, and also a few graphics characters you have defined yourself, perhaps small aliens. You can choose a standard character that is not used frequently, e.g. @ or © and redefine it.

In a word processing situation you may wish to have the character set containing not English characters, but a Greek or Russian alphabet.

To understand how this can be achieved, we need to know how the characters are stored originally. Looking at the memory map shows us that the standard set is stored between locations 46080 and 47104, i.e. they take up 1K (1024) bytes. If there are 128 characters, then each must use up 8 bytes ($128 \times 8 = 1024$). This may lead you to think that they are stored in an 8×8 chess-board

Memory location	Binary Value								Decimal equivalent
46600	0	0	0	0	1	0	0	0	8
46601	0	0	0	1	0	1	0	0	20
46602	0	0	1	0	0	0	1	0	34
46603	0	0	1	0	0	0	1	0	34
46604	0	0	1	1	1	1	1	0	62
46605	0	0	1	0	0	0	1	0	34
46606	0	0	1	0	0	0	1	0	34
46607	0	0	0	0	0	0	0	0	0

arrangement as in some computers. However, this is not quite how ORIC manages it. In each byte, only the last six bits contain character information.

Each character can therefore be thought of as occupying 8 rows of 6 dots. Each row is a byte, of which the last 6 bits determine its design. If a bit is 1 then the cell is "on" and if Ø it is "off".

"On" cells are in foreground colour, "off" cells, are in background.

To look at the contents of any memory position, we use **PEEK**. To change the contents, we use **POKE**.

The characters in the set are stored in the order of their ASCII codes. The ASCII code for **A** is 65, so the pattern for **A** should be stored at 46Ø8Ø + (65*8) i.e. 466ØØ and the next 7 bytes.

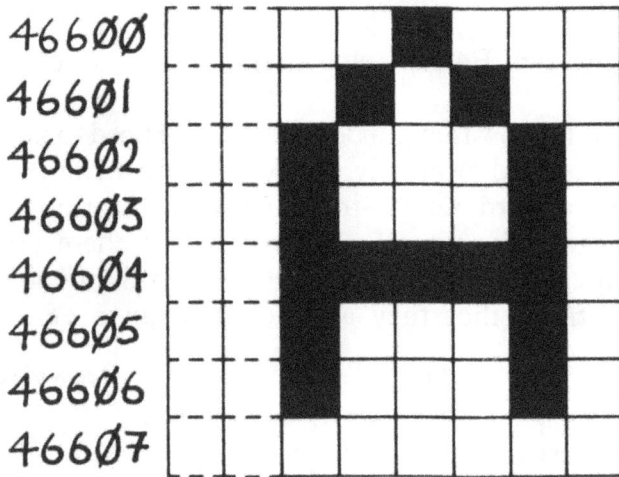

The zeros and ones form a letter A. It is very easy to change it. Try this:

POKE 466ØØ,31
POKE 466Ø1,21
POKE 466Ø2,31
POKE 466Ø3,4
POKE 466Ø4,31
POKE 466Ø5,4
POKE 466Ø6,1Ø
POKE 466Ø7,17

Type **A** now — you have been invaded by ORIC! Any **A** will now appear in its new guise, as you have redefined how ORIC draws an A.

It would take a long time to **POKE** numbers one at a time, so it is better to write a short program to redefine characters.

Here is a frightening program that redefines the entire character set. When you have entered it, **LIST** it, then **RUN** it, and watch the screen. This is total alien domination! The only way to escape from them is to press ORIC's reset button, when you will return to the standard character set.

```
5   REM *** ALIEN DOMINATION ***
10  FOR X = 46344 TO 47088 STEP8
20  FOR I = 0 TO 7
30  READ M
40  POKE I + X,M
50  NEXT I
60  RESTORE
70  NEXT X
80  DATA 18,12,30,45,45,30,18,0
```

Here is a more useful program. You can use it to redefine any keyboard character, upper or lower case. A 2-dimensional array, **Y**, is set up to store the new character in its large form. **C$** is whichever key is pressed. **A** is the start of the standard character set in memory, **D** is the position of the first byte of the chosen character in the standard character set. The subroutine at line 1000 **PEEK**s that byte of the character and converts the decimal contents of that byte into a binary number, i.e. 45 would be converted into 00101101, and either zeros or ones loaded into the array **Y**.

The last section pokes either a solid block (128) if the cell is a 1, or a blank (32) if the cell is a 0 into the screen display. This causes a large version of the character to appear on the screen. The rest of the program gives the user the opportunity to enter fresh data, one line at a time, and to examine the result in actual or enlarged size.

```
5   REM *** CHARACTER GENERATOR ***
10  CLS
20  DIM X(8):DIM Y(8,8)
30  PRINT "PLEASE ENTER THE CHARACTER YOU
    WISH","TO REFEFINE"
```

```
40   GET C$
50   PRINT C$
60   C = ASC(C$)
70   A = 46080:D = C*8
80   GOSUB 1000
90   PRINT"ENTER THE DATA"
100  FOR N = 0 TO 7
110  PRINT"ROW ";N;
120  INPUT X(N)
130  IF X(N)> 63 OR X(N)< 0 THEN 120
140  POKE (A + D + N),X(N)
150  NEXT
160  GOSUB 1000
200  STOP
1000 REM *** CHARACTER GEN.SUBR. ***
1010 FOR N = 0 TO 7
1020 X(N) = PEEK(A + D + N)
1030 FOR M = 0 TO 7
1040 Y(N,M) = INT(X(N)/2⌉(7 - M))
1050 Z = ((X(N)/2⌉(7 - M)) - Y(N,M))*2⌉(7 - M)
1060 X(N) = Z + 0.0001
1070 IF Y(N,M) = 0 THEN POKE 48220 + (N*40) + M,32
1080 IF Y(N,M) = 1 THEN POKE 48220 + (N*40) + M,128
1090 NEXT M
1100 NEXT N
1110 RETURN
```

```
* * * * * * * * *
```

SERIAL ATTRIBUTES

To send information to the screen, ORIC uses serial attributes. This means that a byte sent to the screen can be considered as a graphic pattern or as an attribute controlling colour, flashing, etc.

The way the bits are set determines whether the byte is read as an attribute or not. If bits 6 + 5 are both zero, then the remaining 5 bits are considered as an attribute — there are 32 of these. If bits 6 + 5 are not both zero, then bits 5 to 0 are read as a pattern.

In **HIRES** mode, bits 0 to 5 are the pattern bits. In **TEXT** and **LORES** mode, bits 0 to 6 are the ASCII look up codes. Control codes (bits 6 + 5 set to 0) become attributes. Bit 7 controls whether the character is inverse or not, 1 is on, 0 is off.

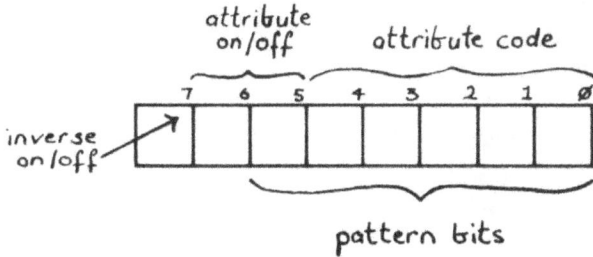

If an attribute is set, then it continues until the end of the line, unless it is reset. To see how serial attributes can be used to control the display in **TEXT** mode, try this program.

```
10  FOR A = 0 TO 255
20  FOR N = 1 TO 24
30  PRINT A;"SOME TEXT TO FILL THE SCREEN"
40  NEXT N
50  FOR J = 48042 TO 49002 STEP 40
60  POKE J,A
70  NEXT J,A
```

Lines 20 to 40 fill the screen with text. Lines 50 + 60 **POKE** variable **A** onto the screen. You should be able to see which values of **A** control colour, flashing, etc. and which result in normal or inverse text being printed. When A is between 24 and 31, the screen will look very strange. This is because you are changing the synchronisation temporarily. See Appendix C for details.

This program demonstrates how serial attributes can control the colour of a predefined characters on the **TEXT** screen.

```
  5  REM **DROPPING ALIENS**
 10  GOSUB 1000:CLS
 20  FOR M = 1 TO 20
 30  PAPER INT(RND(1)*4) + 4
 40  A = RND (1)*32 + 1
 50  ZAP
 60  FOR N = 0 TO 1100 STEP 40
 70  POKE 48039 + N + A, 1
 80  POKE 48040 + N + A, 64
 90  POKE 48039 + N + A + 6, 2
100  POKE 48040 + N + A + 6. 64
```

73

```
110   POKE 48039 + N + A + 3, 3
120   POKE 48040 + N + A + 3, 64
130   SOUND 1,N/2, 0
140   PLAY 1,0,5,5
150   POKE 48040 + N + A, 32
160   POKE 48040 + N + A + 6, 32
170   POKE 48040 + N + A + 3, 32
180   NEXT N
190   EXPLODE
200   WAIT RND(1)*200 + 100
210   NEXT M
1000  REM *** CHARACTER DEFINITION ***
1010  FOR N = 0 TO 7
1020  READ X: POKE 46080 + (64*8) + N,X
1030  NEXT N
1040  DATA 18,12,30,45,45,30,18,0
1050  RETURN
```

You will see from this program that you can have all the foreground colours on the screen at the same time, as well as changing background colours. You do not have to **POKE** into the screen display — **PLOT** will work as well.

Nomally the protected columns on the left of the screen control the **INK** and **PAPER** colours for the whole screen. If you **POKE** an attribute on to the screen, it occupies one character square and effects all the character squares to its right unless you **POKE** another colour attribute after it. As the **INK** attribute is separate to the **PAPER** attribute, it is not necessary to cancel it unless other charactes appear to its right. These would then take on the colour of the closest attribute to their left.

In **HIRES** mode, it is possible to have a colour resolution of 200 lines by 40 character columns. Again, you have to **POKE** the position just to the left of the position you wish to alter.

This program **POKE**s background attributes into the centre of the screen and foreground attributes to the far left. The circles that are drawn take on the colour of the attributes according to their position on the screen.

```
 5   REM ** SPLIT CIRCLE **
10   HIRES
20   FOR N = 41060 TO 48979 STEP 40
30   POKE N,INT (RND(1)*7) + 1
40   POKE N-45,INT (RND(1)*7) + 16
50   NEXT N
60   CURSET 120,100,3
70   FOR X = 95 TO 1 STEP -1
80   CIRCLE X,1
90   NEXT X
```

The second program shows how a graph can have a multicoloured start and then be just one colour for a pre-defined section. You can, of course, **POKE** flashing or double-height attributes on to the screen using this method.

```
 5   REM ** COLOUR SINE **
10   HIRES
20   FOR N = 40960 TO 49079 STEP 40
30   POKE N,INT (RND(1)*7) + 1
40   POKE N + 100,1
50   NEXT N
60   FOR A = -PI TO PI STEP 0.02
70   CURSET A*38 + 120,SIN(A)*99 + 99,1
80   NEXT A
```

CHAPTER 10
Sound

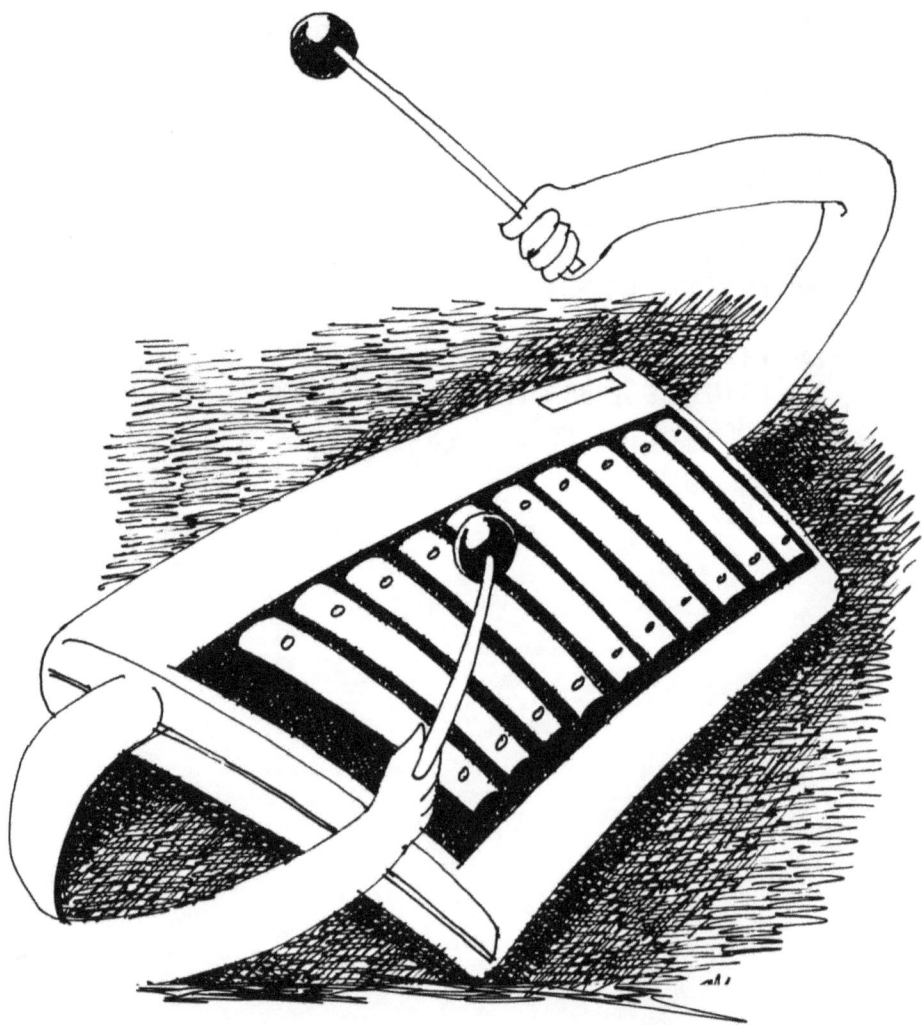

10. Sound

ORIC contains some very sophisticated sound commands, using a specialist chip that can synthesize 3 different tones as well as a noise channel.

You have already experienced some of the sounds available — each time you press a key, ORIC makes a high beep. If you press **CTRL** or [*RETURN*] or any other control keys, you will get a low beep. Try pressing **CTRL** and at the same time press **F**. This will turn off the sound from the keys. If you type **CTRL F** a second time, the sound will return.

Now for some excitement!

Type **ZAP** then [*RETURN*]. This will produce a rapidly falling whistling tone that suggests a 'galactic Laser gun'. Now try **PING** — a bell-like tone that can also be produced by typing **CTRL** and **G**.

SHOOT simulates the sound of a gun being fired. **EXPLODE** generates an explosion.

These are the four predefined sounds that should be useful in arcade action games. They can be put in programs just like any BASIC commands.

```
10   FORN N = 1 TO 10
20   ZAP
30   WAIT 5
40   NEXT N
```

This should fire off a salvo of **ZAP's**.

NOTE:— You must include a pause, as in line 30, to allow the sound to finish before a new one is triggered. The wait length depends on the sound.

The main sound commands are **SOUND, MUSIC** and **PLAY**. In most programs it will be necessary to define the type of sound by the first two commands, and to control the envelope by the third. The envelope determines the "shape" of the sound, i.e. whether it starts sharply, like a guitar-or smoothly, like an organ. These commands will take some time to become familiar with as they offer the chance to make ORIC sound like many existing instruments as well as any you care to invent! "White noise" can be added to give the effects of bombs, planes, etc. The possibilities are limited only by your imagination and are not as complicated as they may appear at first sight.

Here are two short sample programs that will demonstrate some of the things you can do.

```
 5   REM ** MUSIC? **
20   MUSIC 1, RND(1)*6,RND(1)*12+1,7
30   WAIT RND (1)*20+5
40   GOTO 5
```

You can stop execution of this program by typing **CTRL C**. To find out how it works, see the later details that cover the **MUSIC** command.

The next program is a little longer, but it gives you the opportunity to use ORIC as a keyboard instrument. The keys on the top row act to produce notes a semi-tone apart, start at C, and ending with B (the " = " key). Pressing "/" will **STOP** the program. (Always include a **PLAY 0,0,0,0** command at the end or the last note will continue until you hit a key).

```
 5   REM ** KEYBOARD **
20   GET A$
30   A = VAL A$
40   IF A$ = " – " THEN A = 11
50   IF A$ = " = " THEN A = 12
60   IF A$ = "/" THEN PLAY 0,0,0,0: STOP
70   IF A = 0 THEN A = 10
80   MUSIC 1,3,A,5
```

90   GOTO 5

Line 2Ø waits for an input form the keyboard. Line 3Ø reads the value into variable A. If you press a number then A will be the value of that number, if another key, then A will equal Ø. Lines 4Ø to 6Ø convert the remaining keys to the required values. Lie 7Ø stops A from being Ø. (This would result in an error message as the note value in the **MUSIC** command cannot accept Ø as a valid parameter).

Here are the details of the sound commands.

1. SOUND (Channel, Period, Volume)

All the parameters must be numeric. Out of range errors will be detected.

Channel = 1,2 or 3 for tone channels
4,5 or 6 for noise channels

Note that there is only one noise channel, the 4,5 or 6 simply specify which tone channel it is mixed with.

Volume = 1 to 15 fixed volume levels
Ø variable volume level controlled by **PLAY** command

SOUND can be used to produce a wide variety of both musical and non-musical sounds. Channels 1,2 and 3 produce pure tones, and 4,5 and 6 add noise to each tone. The period value controls the pitch, (the name refers to the period of vibration or frequency of the note — do not mistake it for a note length parameter.) Unless you are using an external amplifer, you will probably find that volumes of 6 or 7 are sufficiently loud!

2. MUSIC (Channel, Octave, Note, Volume)

Channel = 1,2 or 3 — tone channels
Octave =   Ø to 6 with Ø giving the lowest tone.
Note =   1 = C Any other numbers will produce an error message.
2 = C $\sharp$
3 = D
4 = D $\sharp$
5 = E
6 = F
7 = F $\sharp$
8 = G

$$9 = G\#$$
$$10 = A$$
$$11 = A\#$$
$$12 = B$$

MUSIC has been designed to offer you pure tones, and the pitch has been set to make it easy to enter notes of a particular value, e.g. from sheet music. There are three available channels, and notes, octave (from 1 to 7), and volume are all selectable.

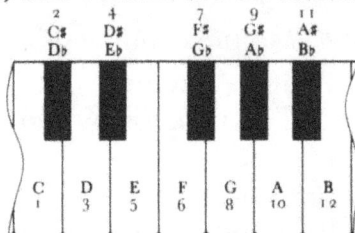

If volume level zero is chosen on **SOUND** or **MUSIC**, then the output is directed to the envelope section of the **PLAY** command. Both **SOUND** and **MUSIC** are switched on by **PLAY**. Note length can be controlled by **WAIT** statements and the sound is switched off by **PLAY 0,0,0,0**.

3. PLAY (Tone Enable, Noise Enable, Envelope Mode, Envelope Period)

Tone Enable =
- 0 = No tone channels on
- 1 = Channel 1 On
- 2 = Channel 2 On
- 3 = Channel 1 + 2 On
- 4 = Channel 3 On
- 5 = Channel 3 + 1 On
- 6 = Channel 3 + 2 On
- 7 = Channel 3 + 2 + 1 On

Noise Enable controls the routing of the noise channel and functions as for **Tone Enable**.

Envelope Mode =

This controls the way the sound is produced i.e. repeating or rise and falling etc.

Envelope Period = Ø to 32767

Controls how long the sound or note takes to start and end.

When you use the sound facilities on ORIC, you may wish to turn off the keyboard click by pressing **CTRL** and **F** once. If it is left on, then key presses may affect the sound output.

This program illustrates one way in which note values, both in terms of pitch and length, may be held in **DATA** statements and called when required during the execution of the program. A chord effect is achieved by opening channels 1 and 2 in the **PLAY** statement.

```
10    REM ** TUNE **
20    FOR N = 1 TO 11
30    READ A,B
40    MUSIC2,3,A,Ø
45    PLAY3,Ø,7,2ØØØ
50    WAIT B
60    PLAY Ø,Ø,Ø,Ø
80    NEXT N
100   DATA 5,3Ø,5,3Ø,7,3Ø,8,75,5,75
110   DATA 8,6Ø,1Ø,3Ø,7,6Ø,5,3Ø,3,3Ø,5,18Ø
```

Although **MUSIC** and **SOUND** are fairly easy to imagine in terms of the sounds they will produce, **PLAY** is more difficult.

This program allows you to enter the different channels, 1,2 and 3, and also to alter the two envelope parameters, mode and period. In this way, you will soon become familiar with all the sound commands that ORIC has to offer.

```
5     REM ** ENVELOPE TEST **
10    INPUT "ENTER THE TONE CHANNEL- 1,2OR
      3";T
20    IF T< 1 OR T> 3 THEN 10
30    INPUT "ENTER THE ENVELOPE MODE, Ø TO
      7";M
40    IF M< Ø OR M> 7 THEN 30
50    INPUT "ENTER THE ENVELOPE PERIOD, Ø TO
      32767";P
```

```
 60   IF P< 0 OR P> 32767 THEN 50
 70   CLS
 80   PRINT "CHANNEL "T
 90   PRINT "ENVELOPE MODE "M
100   PRINT "ENVELOPE PERIOD "P
110   MUSIC T,3,4,0
120   PLAY T,0,M,P
130   PRINT "PRESS RETURN IF SOUND CONTINUES"
```

CHAPTER 11
Saving programs on tape

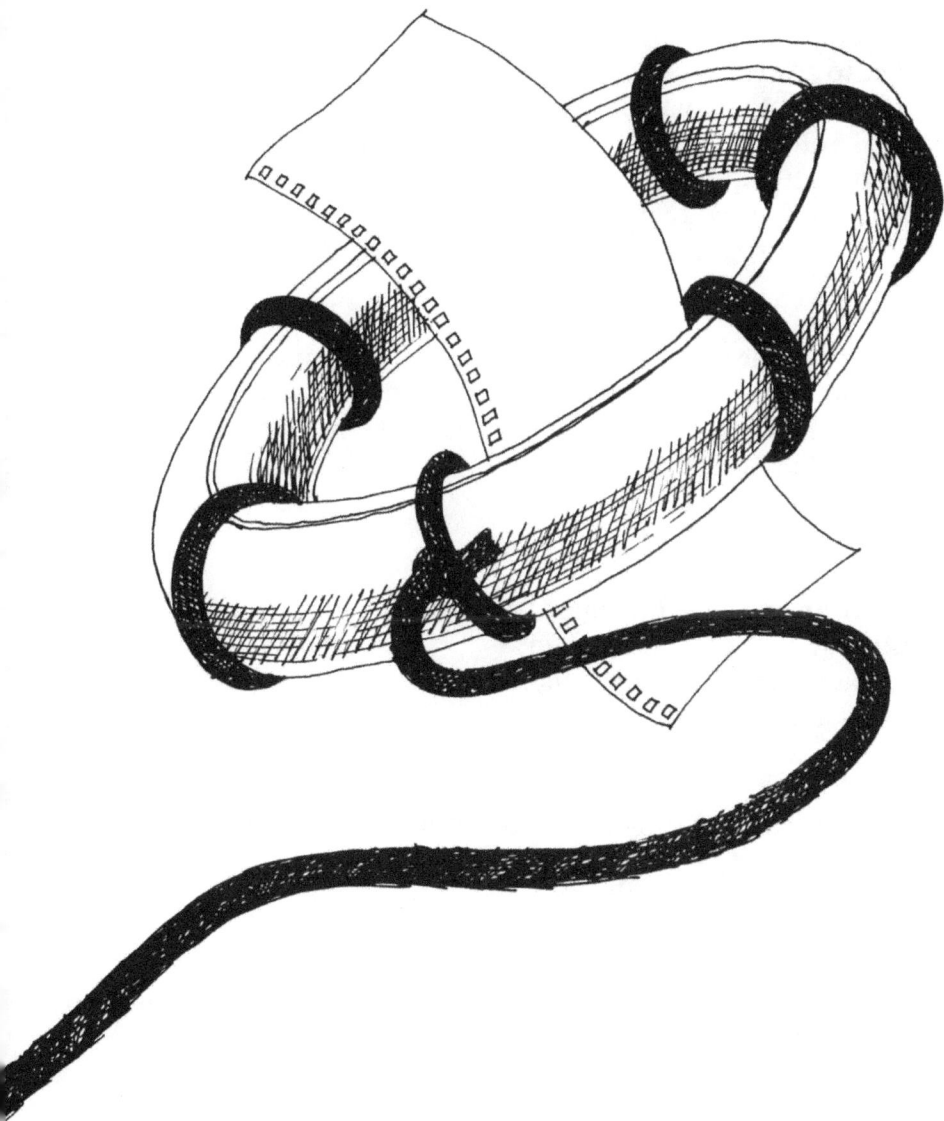

11. Saving programs on tape

When you have spent some time typing in a long program, it's nice to know that you can store your program away somewhere and load it into ORIC or another ORIC at a later stage.

You will need a cassette recorder and a connecting lead to do this. As mentioned previously, the plugs depend on the type of recorder you have. ORIC has a 7-pin socket at the back for cassette input/output. If your recorder has a "remote" socket, it can be connected to the extra pins. (If not, don't worry — a 3 pin DIN plug should fit, but you will have to remember to switch the machine on and off yourself, or use the **PAUSE** button).

Do not attempt to use a 5 pin DIN plug, as the outer pairs of pins are usually shorted together and will not function on ORIC.

To save a program, switch the recorder on to record and type

CSAVE "XX"

(XX is the name you give to your program and may be up to 17 characters in length and include full stops, hyphens, etc.) When you press [**RETURN**], the program will be converted into sound signals and recorded on the tape.

The message

Saving XX

will appear on the status line. When the program has been saved, **Ready** will appear on the screen.

To load the program back in, make sure the recorder is connected properly and type

CLOAD "XX"

ORIC will search through the tape until it reaches program "**XX**" and will then load it into internal memory.

While it is searching, the message

Searching. . . .

will appear on the status line. When the required program has been found, the message will change to

Loading XX

If you have forgotten the program name, or simply wish to load in the next program on the cassette, then type

CLOAD""

You can buy special computer data cassettes that are not very long — C10 or C15 — or you can use good quality audio cassettes. Short cassettes are preferable as it is easier to locate a program.

A final warning — don't try and record on the plastic leader at the start of the tape. Your ears may not mind missing half a note at the start of some music, but ORIC will complain if even one byte is missing!

As well as saving programs normally, ORIC allows you to be far more versatile in the use of your recorder. If you **CSAVE** programs as above, they are recorded at the fast rate of 2400 baud (a measure of data transfer). You should find that this speed is perfectly reliable provided the record/replay head on the cassette recorder is clean and well-aligned, and you are using good quality tapes.

If there is a fault in the tape, you may get the error message

FILE ERROR — LOAD ABORTED

If you wish to be absolutely sure that your masterpiece is **CSAVE**d for posterity, then you may add the letter **S** to the **CSAVE** instruction as follows, which will transfer data at the super reliable speed of 300 baud.

CSAVE "PROG 1",S

When you **CLOAD** slow programs, you must type **CLOAD** **"PROG 1",S** or ORIC will expect a fast load.

If you wish your program to **RUN** automatically once it has been loaded, add the instruction **AUTO** to the **CSAVE** instruction.

CSAVE "PROG 1",AUTO

There is no need to add anything to the instruction when an auto-run program is **CLOAD**ed.

CLOAD "PROG1"

will **RUN** immediately after loading, as the **AUTO** message is encoded with the program on the tape.

To save blocks of memory, you need to know the **A**ddress where the block starts, and where it **E**nds, as follows.

CSAVE "PROGMEM", A ‖400, E ‖499

This would save the contents of **RAM** held from locations ‖400 to ‖499.
To load the block back, type

CLOAD "PROGMEM", A ‖400,E ‖499

Because the rest of **RAM** is unaffected, it is possible to load in new character sets, machine code programs, etc., without corrupting the Basic program.

You can also use this method to save the screen displays, and load them back in at a later date. Make sure if you use this method, that you are in the same mode that the display needs, or strange things may happen!

To save the **TEXT** or **LORES** screen, type

CSAVE "NICEPICCY1",A48000,E49119.

Note that you can use decimal or hexadecimal numbers for the locations. All the additional commands may be used together in any order, e.g.

CSAVE "AVON",S,A ‖400,E ‖420

CHAPTER 12
Better Basic

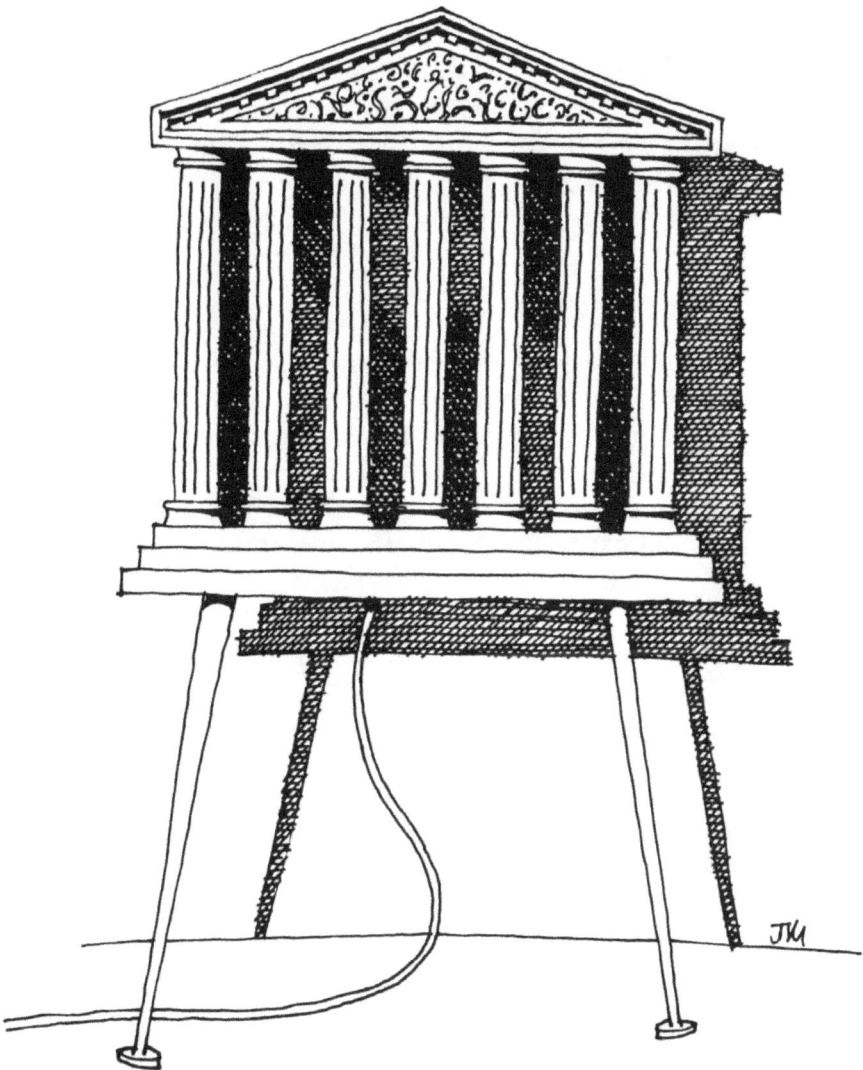

12. Better Basic

Up until this point, you may have felt quite confident about using ORIC. You will be copying programs from books and magazines and probably starting to write your own original programs too.

This chapter is designed to help you improve your program writing and to make the most of the considerable facilities available on ORIC.

The short example programs in this manual do not take up much memory. When you switch on, you are told how much memory is available for you to fill with programs. Some of this will be used by the **TEXT** screen, and rather more if you are in **HIRES** mode. Some more memory will be used to store variables, etc. To find out the memory you have left, type

PRINT FRE (0)

The number of bytes left will be printed.

If you write longer programs, each time a string variable is used, it is copied into an extra part of the memory. This is particularly noticeable in long **FOR/NEXT** loops, or in nested subroutines. If you start to run out of memory, it may be useful to clear out all the extra copies — after all, only the most recent one is needed. This is sometimes referred to as "house-keeping" or as "garbage-collection". Although a certain amount is automatic, you can force garbage-collection by having a line such as

240   A = FRE ("")

in the necessary part of the program.

When you write small programs, they are easy to compose at the keyboard. Any problems are fairly easy to sort out, and you can probably tell what the program does by glancing at the listing.

With programs longer than about 20 lines or so, this gets progressively more difficult, and a week later you may wonder how you got it to work in the first place, and to anyone else it may appear totally incomprehensible.

There are several ways in which you may make your program clearer to yourself and to others. These are not hard and fast rules, but they will undoubtedly improve your programming and also make it easier if you decide to move on to other languages, such as Pascal or Forth.

First of all, it is a good idea to write down your ideas for the program on paper, rather than attempt to work them out at the keyboard. This does not have to be in the form of a traditional flowchart; indeed, flowcharts should not be necessary for well-designed programs. Something simple to show the order of events is all that is needed.

As an example, imagine that you have been asked to write a program that will demonstrate how straight lines can appear as a smooth curve. This effect is often called Curve Stitching.

This is the effect.

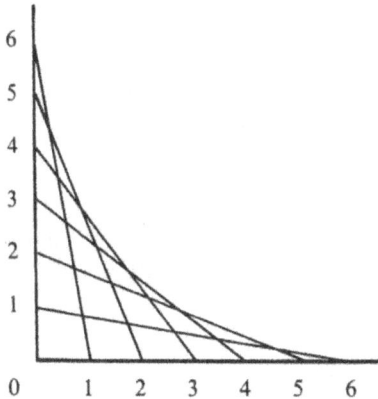

The flow of control is like this:—

**RUN → INITIALIZE → INSTRUCTIONS →
MAIN PROGRAM → REPEAT OPTION**

Instructions have been included so that anyone else using the program will know what it does and how to operate it. Taking the needs of the user first is often termed an "outside-in" approach.

Each section of the program will be written as a separate module and each module will be called as a separate subroutine in the order given above. At the beginning will be a control module to call the subroutines. This is the module that is written first.

```
2000    REM ** CONTROL MODULE **
2010    GOSUB 3000  'INITIALIZATION
2020    GOSUB 4000  'INSTRUCTIONS
2030    GOSUB 5000  'MAIN PROGRAM
2040    STOP
```

The program is now effectively written! All that is necessary is for the subroutines to be filled in. In practice, you may find you have subroutines already written that will be suitable. It is quite useful to build up a library of these.

At this stage, you will find it helpful to use the computer to test the modules. These will be introduced one at a time.

* * * * * * * * *

INITIALIZATION.

When you switch on ORIC, all variables are set to zero. This means that you do not need to give variables initial values if they need the value of zero in the program, although it is a good idea to use names and letters that remind you of what they stand for e.g:—

SIZE = 160 (length of square in pixels).

Be careful you do not have two variables that start with the same two letters. You must also avoid reserved words, like **KEY** or **LET** which are already in Basic.

If you put **REM** statements at the beginning of subroutines and next to variables, you will be able to see at a glance what they do. e.g:—

I = RND(1)*7 :REM **CHOOSES INK COLOUR AT RANDOM

* * * * * * * *

THE MAIN MODULE.

When you reach the main section of the progam, then if it involves graphics it is useful to sketch the finished display on paper and work out which values will keep the lines within the screen boundaries.

How will the display be built up? It is possible to define each line on the screen one at a time, but this is wasteful on memory and hardly elegant. If you know the starting position of the lines and the step size, it is better to use **FOR/NEXT** loops.

In this program, it is possible to use two **FOR/NEXT** loops nested inside one another.

REPEAT
  FOR INCR = 31 TO 3 STEP − 2
    FOR COUNT = 0 TO SIZE STEP INCR
      DRAW ROUTINE
    NEXT COUNT
  NEXT INCR
UNTIL KEY$ < > ""

These loops are held within a **REPEAT . . . . UNTIL** loop that controls the repeat option. Notice that the loops do not overlap, and that you can only enter and leave each loop by one path.

There is another feature of ORIC that can be usefully employed here. This is called program indenting. Normally, any leading spaces are lost by ORIC, so if you enter

    10   PRINT A

the listing will show

    10   PRINT A

If however, you enter a semi-colon first, there will be no difference in program execution, but leading spaces after the semi- colon will remain.

Using this feature, you can indent all the loop structures in your program. Although this takes more time, the programs will be easier to understand. Several of the programs in the manual are indented to make their structure clear. They will of course work with the semi-colons and indenting removed.

As has been previously mentioned, it is usual to space program lines 1Ø apart to allow for additions at a later date.

To complete your program, it needs a title, as well as your name and the date upon which you completed that particular version. This makes it clear to you and anyone else what you intend the program to do and it reminds you when you wrote it.

At a later date you may acquire a printer. Listings produced by this means will look much neater, and your programs therefore easier to decipher if they are neatly indented.

Deciding on a program and building it up in this manner is called top-down programming. Building one up from program lines is called, naturally enough, bottom-up.

Top-down programming produces a clearly-defined structure. It also means that you rarely use **GOTO** statements. Although they appear initially to be the programmer's friend, their unrestricted use all over your programs will make them difficult to understand and lead to that unpleasant syndrome, "spaghetti programming".

```
1Ø   PRINT "ENTER THE DATA"
2Ø   INPUT A
3Ø   IF A = 3Ø THEN GOTO 5Ø
4Ø   GOTO 1Ø
5Ø   GOTO 7Ø
6Ø   PRINT A;" WAS MORE THAN 1ØØ":STOP
7Ø   PRINT A;" WAS THE LAST NUMBER"
8Ø   IF A> 1ØØ THEN GOTO 6Ø
9Ø   END
```

This is rather an extreme example, but it does demonstrate how confusing unstructured programs can be. Use of **REPEAT/UNTIL, FOR/NEXT** and **IF/THEN....ELSE** will help you avoid falling into a tub of spaghetti!

Here, then, is the completed curve stitching program. It is not offered as the most wonderful program ever written, simply as an example of how the use of loops, **REMs** and indenting can improve the look of a program.

```
1ØØØ   :REM ** CURVE STITCHING **
1Ø1Ø   :REM
```

```
1020   :REM ** COPYRIGHT A.J.S. **
1030   :REM
1040   :REM ** 1/1/83 **
1050   :REM
2000   :REM ** CONTROL MODULE **
2010   :GOSUB 3000   'INITIALIZATION
2020   :GOSUB 4000   'INSTRUCTIONS
2030   :GOSUB 5000   'MAIN PROGRAM
2040   :STOP
2050   :REM
3000   :REM ** INITIALIZATION **
3010   :REM
3020   :INK1:PAPER 4
3030   :SIZE = 160
3040   :TEXT
3050   :RETURN
3060   :REM
4000   :REM ** INSTRUCTIONS **
4010   :REM
4020   :CLS
4025   :B$ = "L        ****CURVE STITCHING****"
4030   :PRINT CHR$(27);B$
4032   :PRINT
4034   :PRINT
4035   :PRINT
4036   :PRINT
4040   :PRINT "This program will draw lines from"
4045   :PRINT "each side of a square to adjacent"
4050   :PRINT "sides. The step size is the distance"
4055   :PRINT "each line is from its neighbour."
4060   :PRINT "As each set is completed the square"
4065   :PRINT "will be redrawn with the step size"
4070   :PRINT "reduced by two."
4080   :PRINT
4090   :PRINT "Press RETURN to start"
4100   :GET A$
4110   :RETURN
4120   :REM
5000   :REM ** MAIN PROGRAM **
```

```
5010  :REM
5020  :REPEAT
5030  :   FOR INCR = 31 TO 3 STEP − 2
5040  :   HIRES
5050  :      PRINT "STEP" INCR
5060  :      INK (INCR/6)+1
5070  :      FOR COUNT = 0 TO SIZE STEP INCR
5080  :         CURSET 180-COUNT,10,3
5090  :         DRAW COUNT,SIZE-COUNT,1
5100  :         CURSET 20,COUNT+10,3
5110  :         DRAW COUNT,SIZE-COUNT,1
5120  :         CURSET COUNT+20,170,3
5130  :         DRAW SIZE-COUNT,-COUNT,1
5140  :         CURSET 20,COUNT+10,3
5150  :         DRAW SIZE-COUNT,-COUNT,1
5160  :      NEXT COUNT
5170  :      WAIT 100
5180  :   NEXT INCR
5190  :PRINT "PRESS ANY KEY TO STOP":WAIT
      500
5200  :UNTIL KEY$ < > ""
5210  :RETURN
```

Structured programming does have its drawbacks and you will have to decide when it is too wasteful on memory. Some people keep a master copy of a program separately, complete with **REM** statements, and explanations of how it works, while the working copies have the **REMs** and indenting removed. It is always useful to be able to refer to the master copy if you need to alter the program at a later date.

Advantages of a structured approach.
1. The flow of control is easy to follow.
2. The structures will fit into neat, separate modules.
3. The numbers of mistakes will be reduced, and those errors that do creep in are easily eliminated.
4. The ideas inherent in this approach make learning other languages and their application much easier.

Disadvantages.
1. Structured programs may use more memory.
2. The speed of the program may be reduced.
3. The hardware of the computer may not be used in the most economical manner.
4. It is harder to learn to write good structured programs than it is to pick up sloppy habits!

Mug-trapping.
Writing structured programs may make you a better programmer, but it is no guarantee that your program is as good as it could be. When you test your pièce de résistance, then if it is designed to be used by others it is important to consider all the silly things they may decide to enter.

If you ask for a number to be input, what happens if a user enters "two" instead of "2"? What happens if they press **RETURN** without entering anything?

Luckily, ORIC is kind to errant users. In the first instance — a string being entered instead of a number — **REDO FROM START** will be printed until a figure is input. In the second case, ORIC will wait until something is actually entered. If **RETURN** is constantly pressed, then the question mark prompt will constantly re-appear.

You can make your requirements easier for the user to understand. If you check the ASCII code of the input, or the value of a number, then a message telling the user what to enter can be built into your program.

```
10   INPUT "ENTER THE YEAR";A$
20   IF VAL(A$) < 1900 OR VAL(A$) > 1985 THEN
     PRINT "BETWEEN 1900 & 1985,
     PLEASE":GOTO 100
30   PRINT "THANKS!"
```

If you draw a line or move a character, it is important not to go off the edge of the screen or to print it in one of the protected columns. You may realise this, but another user may not.

If A is the horizontal position and B the vertical position on the **HIRES** screen, then something like this may help.

```
If A > 238 THEN A = 238
IF A < 1 THEN A = 1
IF B > 198 THEN B = 198
IF B < 1 THEN B = 1
```

This should be useful provided the character is no larger than two pixels. Change the values according to your requ irements.

You have to imagine the worst thing anyone could do to your program, and even then it's more likely that someone, somewhere will be able to crash it. There is no such thing as a perfect program, but it is possible to "error-trap", "mug-trap" or "idiot-proof" your program to a fair degree. You will then have what is more politely termed, a robust program.

CHAPTER 13
Machine code programs

13. Machine code programs

It has been mentioned previously that computers do not yet understand normal English commands, as these are ambiguous as well as idiosyncratic. The best they can do is interpret a language like Basic that approaches to some degree, a limited sub-set of English.

Computer languages can be seen as a hierarchy, with those that are close to natural language at the top — high level languges — and the binary code of machine language — low level — at the bottom.

The high level language that is supplied with ORIC is Basic. The chip that translates Basic into machine code is called the Basic ROM. ROM stands for Read Only memory, and the interpreter program it contains is fixed during manufacture, and cannot be altered. If you have a 48K model, it actually contains 64K of RAM (Random Access Memory that can be changed, and usually holds your programs).

If you purchase disc drives for large, fast memory storage, the internal ROM is masked out, leaving nearly 64K of internal memory. In this way, other high level language, such as Forth, Pascal, Logo, Prolog and Lisp could be used with ORIC.

With all this potential for high level languages, that are much clearer to understand, you may wonder why anyone should bother with machine code. After all, it is estimated that it takes at least ten times as long to write as the equivalent program in a high-level language. You do not get helpful error messages, faults are much more difficult to trace, and machine code is difficult to document and difficult to understand — so why attempt to learn it?

An understanding of machine code will help you undertand the workings of computers, and efficient machine code programs are executed at a much faster rate than any high-level language. If you imagine speaking to a German, who in turn translates your instructions to an Italian before a job is carried out, and you will see the advantage of being able to speak to the Italian in his own language!

There are several ways in which machine languages can be made more comprehensible. Firstly, it is usually written in hexadecimal — a page of binary soon blurs into a mass of zeros and ones, and decimal numbers do not readily show you what is happening at byte level.

This is why the facility is provided on ORIC to enter numbers in either decimal or hexadecimal form, rather than wasting time doing base conversions. It also provides a code that is easier to read.

In the heart of ORIC is the most important chip, the central processor unit.

All computers need a C.P.U. but they do not all use the same model. Any other computer that uses the same C.P.U. can, within the limits of the computer, use the same machine code program. ORIC uses a 6502 processor from Rockwell International Corporation. Other processors you may come across are 6800, 6809, Z80 and 8080. These all operate in slightly different ways, so understand different instructions.

Internally, the processor manipulates numbers, stored as 8-bit binary digits. Numbers are loaded into different memory locations and treated either as instructions or as data.

For instance, if the 6502 receives the number 10101001, it understands this to be an instruction: load a register, or special memory store called the accumulator with the next number received. The 6502 only understands 8-bit numbers. ORIC allows you to enter decimal or hex numbers, and converts them into their binary equivalent before sending them to the 6502.

To make it easier to remember, a short name is given to each 6502 instruction, so in the previous example, 10101001, or 169 (decimal) or # A9 (hex) is known as LDA (LoaD Accumulator). These memory-joggers are called mnemonics. To assist you in using machine code in ORIC, there is a section in the appendices on 6502 mnemonics.

Although entering A9 into ORIC would be understood, the mnemonic would not be recognised. To make it clearer, it could be added as a **REM** statement, e.g.

100 DATA # A9, # 20 'LDA # 20

To aid you in entering machine code programs, it is possible to have a short program that will allow you to enter mnemonics directly, as well as variables, data and addresses, etc., and it will decode this into machine language. This is called an assembler program. The user enters the mnemonics (the "source" program) and the assembler translates this into a machine code or "object" program. A disassembler program works in reverse.

* * * * * * * * *

PEEK AND POKE

How can we tell what is stored in any memory location? You may remember coming across **PEEK** and **POKE** in previous chapters. Type:—

PRINT PEEK (48225)

This is looking into the part of memory that is used to store the **TEXT** screen. The number return is the decimal equivalent of the binary number stored at that location. As this location is mapped to the screen area, the number is the ASCII code for the character at that position. To change that value, type:—

POKE 48225,128

You should be able to see which position on your screen 48225 controls, as it will be filled with the character represented by ASCII 128, i.e. a solid block.

If you look at the memory map in the appendix, you will see what is stored at different locations. You can try using **POKE** to put characters on the **TEXT** and **HIRES** screen.

This technique has already been used in the graphics chapter. It is not a good idea to try to **POKE** into pages Ø to 3 (Ø to 1Ø24 in decimal). You can of course experiment, as you will not damage ORIC, whatever you enter.

* * * * * * * * *

ADDRESSES

Perhaps you have wondered how ORIC can store numbers larger than 255, particularly as there are 65536 different memory locations. Addresses are stored as two byte numbers. e.g.

	1st byte	2nd byte
128 is stored as	1ØØØØØØØ	ØØØØØØØØ

If the number is greater than 255, the second byte contains the number of 256's in the number.

e.g. 258 is stored as

	1st byte	2nd byte
	ØØØØØØ1Ø	ØØØØØØØ1
	2 +	(1 × 256)

It may seem strange that the low order byte comes first, but that is the order in which the processor decodes it. So, if you know a number is stored at locations 20345 and 20346, to calculate the number stored would require you to type:

PRINT PEEK (20345) + (PEEK(20346)*256)

ORIC saves you having to do this. The instruction

PRINT DEEK (20345)

will do the same job as the line above. **DEEK** stands for Double **PEEK**. If you wished to change the number held in those two locations, you would type

DOKE 20345, N

and **N** would be converted into a two byte number.

* * * * * * * * *

Sometimes it is useful to be able to use short machine code routines, although the rest of your program may be written in Basic. These can be totally original, or you can borrow routines that are already written into ROM by **PEEK**ing.

There are several commands in ORIC BASIC that allow you to do this.

CALL X, where **X** is an address in memory, transfers control to the address specified and begins the machine code routine that is held there. Return to Basic is accomplished when the routine reaches an **RTS**. (ReTurn from Subroutine).

Another way of accessing information from a machine code routine is to use **DEF USR** and **PRINT USR (0)**. The routine is written in machine code and the start address is entered by **DEF USR** = start address.

If **PRINT USR (0)** is now entered, the result of the routine is extracted from the floating-point accumulator and printed. Here is an example of how it can be used:

```
  5   REM *** RAD/DEG CONSTANT ***
 10   FOR DISP = 0 TO 12
 20   : READ DTA
 30   : POKE # 400 + DISP,DTA
 40   NEXT DISP
100   DATA # A9, # 07        'LDA # CON57 ;LO
110   DATA # A0, # 04        'LDA # CON57 ;HI
120   DATA # 4C, # 73, # DE  'JMP MOVFM ;FLOAT.
130   DATA # 86, # 65, # 2E, # E0, # D8
                             'CONSTANT180/PI
```

RUN the program, then type **DEF USR** = # 400 At any time, **PRINT USR (0)** will print out the conversion constant for radians to degrees.

Here is a more detailed explanation of how it operates. The value held in brackets after the **USR** function is actually passed to the floating-point accumulator and a **JSR** to location # 21 is performed. Locations # 21 to # 23 must contain a **JMP** to the beginning location of the machine language subroutine. The return value for the function is placed in the floating-point accumulator.

To obtain a 2-byte integer from the value in the floating-point accumulator, the subroutine should do a **JSR** to # D867. Upon return, the integer value will be in locations # 34 (high-order byte) and # 33 (low-order byte).

If you wish to convert an integer result to its floating-point equivalent, so that the function can return that value, the two byte integer must be placed in registers A(high-order byte) and Y(low-order byte). If a **JSR** is done to # D8D5, then upon return, the floating-point value will have been loaded into the floating-point accumulator.

There are two other useful operations that ORIC can perform.
! can be defined as a command that does not already exist in ORIC Basic.
& (X) (where X = 0 to # FFFF)
can be defined as a function that does not already exist in ORIC Basic.

The routines have to be written in machine code and loaded into a particular location in memory. The start address is loaded as follows:

102

DOKE # **2F5**, address — start address of ! routine.
DOKE # **2FC**, address — start address of & routine.
To define ! to mean **PRINT AT** type:—

```
  5   REM ***** PROGRAM FOR EXTENSION CMD FOR
      'PRINT @ X,Y ;JJJJ'.
 10   REPEAT
 20   READ DTA
 30   POKE # 400 + CL,DTA
 40   CL = CL + 1
 50   UNTIL DTA = # FF          :REM END OF PROG.
100   DATA # 20, # 96, # D9     :REM JSR GTVALS
110   DATA # AC, # F8, # 0/2    :REM LDY GCOL
120   DATA # C8                 :REM INY
130   DATA # 8C, # 69, # 02     :REM STY CURCOL
140   DATA # A5, # 1F           :REM LDA GCL
150   DATA # A4, # 20           :REM LDY GHC
160   DATA # 85, # 12           :REM STA CURBAS
170   DATA # 84, # 13           :REM STY CURBAS + 1
180   DATA # A9, # 3B           :REM LDA # ';'
190   DATA # 20, # DB, # CF     :REM JSR SYNCHR
200   DATA # 4C, # 61, # CB     :REM JMP PRINT
210   DATA # FF
220   DOKE # 2F5, # 400
```

If you type:

!X,Y;"ORIC"

then ORIC will be printed at co-ordinates X and Y on the screen.
To define **&** to mean *RETURN VERTICAL CURSOR POSITION:*—

```
  5   REM ** EXTENSION CMD VERT/CURS/POS
 10   FOR N = 0 TO 5
 20   READ DTA
 30   POKE # 400 + N, DTA
 40   NEXT
 50   DOKE # 2FC, # 400
 60   DATA # AC, # 68, # 02
 70   DATA # 4C, # FD, # D3
```

103

It is useful to know which line the cursor is on if you need to use the double height feature, so you do not end up with tops of letters under their bottom halves.

A suitable line in a program to protect against this would be

500 IF & (0)/2< > INT(&(0)/2) THEN PRINT

This will move the cursor down to an even line.

Some of page 4 (locations # 0400 to # 0420) has been reserved for your own machine code routines. Anywhere in memory may be used for longer programs, but a Basic program may over-write it if it occupies the *USER PROGRAMS* space in RAM.

To reserve memory for machine code programs, the top of the user area can be lowered. To find its present position, enter

PRINT DEEK(# A6)

Work out how many bytes you require for your program, add on a small number for safety (unless you are really pushed for memory), and subtract the total from the number you previously found. Then enter

HIMEM X

where X is the new top of user memory you have just calculated.

If you wish to learn more about using 6502 machine code, then there are several books which cover the subject in great detail.

Some of the more useful ones are written by Rodnay Zaks (published by Sybex) and Lance Leventhal (published by Osborne McGraw-Hill). Other information and books can be obtained from Rockwell International themselves.

CHAPTER 14
Using a printer

14. Using a printer

Oric may be used with any printer that has a Centronics interface. As well as the printer, you will need a connecting cable. The printer connection is located at the back, next to the expansion port.

The printer should be connected before switching on. If all is well the printing head should align itself at the starting position as soon as power is supplied. In addition to the instruction booklet with the printer, you may find the following information helpful.

On first connecting the printer, run the following program.

```
10   REM  ** PRINTER TEST **
20   FOR N = 0 TO 255
30   LPRINT N,CHR$(N)
40   NEXT N
```

When you have entered the program type

LLIST

This will list the program on the printer instead of on the screen. If you do not get a listing, but merely Japanese or graphics characters, consult the printer handbook as to changing the character set in the printer. When the listing is satisfactory run the program.

As you can see, it consists of a simple loop that will **LPRINT** (print to the printer, rather than to the screen) the number followed by the Ascii character that represents that code. This will show you the character set available and, just as importantly, will show you which numbers are read as control codes on the printer.

Although these are standardised to a certain extent, not all printers respond in the same manner. The control codes determine actions such as line feed, carriage return, form feed, character size, etc.

For example, Microline printers will print standard, compressed or expanded characters. If you were to type

LPRINT CHR$(31)

then subsequent characters on the printer would be twice their normal size — very useful for headings etc.

LPRINT CHR$(30)

would result in a return to normal print.

LPRINT CHR$(12)

results in a form feed on Dec-writers. (The paper feeds through to the bottom of the page) These codes are useful to know as they can be incorporated in your programs.

Many printers that have graphic characters will also dump the contents of the screen on to the printer which is a way to get a permanent record of pictures etc.

You will probably find a printer most useful in producing listing s so you can see the structure of a complete program. They are also essential for getting hard copy of electronic mail.

CHAPTER 15
Oric Basic

15. ORIC Basic

COMMAND	EFFECT	EXAMPLE
ABS	Returns absolute value	**ABS(– 4) is 4**
		ABS(4) is 4
ASC	Returns ASCII code of first character in string. See appendix.	**A = ASC(N$)**
ATN	Returns arctangent in radians.	**Z = ATN(Y/4)**
CALL	Transfers control to machine code routine starting at address X. Return to Basic on reaching an RTS.	**CALL X**
CHAR	Draws a character at current cursor position — top left of character is at cursor position. X is ASCII code (32–127), S is either Ø, standard character set or 1, alternate character set. FB is Ø to 3 (see below).	**CHAR X,S,FB**
CHR$	Returns the ASCII character that corresponds to the value (32–128).	**CHR$(value)**
CIRCLE	Draws a circle centred at current cursor position. No part of the circle may leave the screen. R is the radius (1–119) FB is Ø to 3 (see below).	**CIRCLE R,FB**
CLEAR	Sets variables to Ø, and strings to null (empty).	**CLEAR**
CLS	Clears screen display.	**CLS**
CLOAD	Loads file name XX from tape. For additional tape commands, see Chapter 11.	**CLOAD "XX"**
CONT	Continues execution of program after break.	**CONT**

NOTE:— FB Codes. FB is foreground/background value

Ø	Background	2	Invert
1	Foreground	3	Null (do nothing).

COS	Returns cosine of angle N (N must be in radians).	**A = COS(N)**
CURMOV	Sets the cursor to a new position. X,Y are relative to old position. FB is 0−3 (see below).	**CURMOV X, Y,FB**
CURSET	Sets the cursor to absolute X,Y position. Note:— final position of X must be 0 to 239, and Y 0 to 199 in all graphics commands. FB is 0−3.	**CURSET X,Y, FB**
CSAVE	Saves file name XX to tape.	
DATA	Stores a list of data that can be READ into variables. May include numeric and string variables. Leading spaces will be lost unless enclosed by quotes.	**DATA 1,2, BATH, " ANGIE"**
DEEK	Returns the contents of byte plus 256 times of the contents of next byte.	**?DEEK(45610)**
DEF FN	Defines numeric functions.	**DEF FNA(Z) = Z + 4**
DEF USR	Defines start of USR routine.	**DEF USR = # 400**
DIM	Dimensions arrays. (Arrays are predimensioned to 10).	**DIM A$(10,5)**
DOKE	Stores value V in locations X and X + 1. INT(V/256) goes in X + 1, and the remainder in X.	**DOKE X,V**
DRAW	Draws a vector from current cursor to current cursor plus X,Y. FB is 0−3.	**DRAW X,Y,FB**
END	Ends program.	**END**
EXP	Returns natural exponential of N.	**A = EXP(N)**
EXPLODE	Produces predefined sound.	**EXPLODE**
FALSE	Returns a value of 0.	
FILL	Fills A character cells by B rows with N value. There are 200 rows and 40 character cells. N must be an integer between 0 and 127.	**FILL B,A,N**

110

FN	Produces the result of a predefined function.	**PRINT FNA(X)**
FOR....TO STEP/NEXT	Creates a loop to repeat all program lines between FOR and NEXT. STEP determines the incremental size. If omitted, 1 is used.	**FOR N = 1 TO NEXT N**
FRE	Returns the amount of memory available in bytes.	**FRE(0)**
	Also:—	
	Forces variable garbage-collection.	**FRE("")**
GET	Strobes the keyboard and waits until a key is pressed.	**GET A$**
GOSUB	Causes program branch to line number specified. See RETURN.	**GOSUB 1000**
GOTO	Unconditional branch to line number specified.	**GOTO 4000**
GRAB	Assigns the area in memory from #9800 to #B400 (48K) or from #1800 to #3400 (16K) to user RAM (See memory map).	**GRAB**
HEX$	Prints the value V as a hexa-decimal number.	**PRINT HEX$(V)**
HIMEM	Lowers top of memory available for BASIC programs. Memory above may then be used for machine code programs.	**HIMEM # 8700**
HIRES	Switches to high-resolution mode. Background is set to black, foreground to white, cursor to 0,0 Text lines remain in existing colours.	**HIRES**
IF/THEN ....ELSE	If the expression following IF is true, then executes all instructions following THEN. If the expression is false, then these instructions are ignored and program executes instructions following ELSE. ELSE may be omitted.	**IF A> 10 THEN PRINT "OK"**

111

INK	Changes foreground colour of whole screen. N is an integer 0-7.	**INK N**
INPUT	Stops program execution and waits for an input before continuing.	**INPUT N$** **INPUT "Age? ";A**
INT	Returns largest integer less than or equal to value in brackets.	**X = INT(Y + 0.5)**
KEY$	Strobes keyboard. Continues execution, whether or not a key has been pressed. X$ contains value of any key pressed.	**X$ = KEY$**
LEFT$	Returns the left portion of a string, N characters in length.	**L$ = LEFT$ (A$,N)**
LEN	Returns the length of a string.	**A = LEN(N$)**
LET	Assigns value to a variable. (Optional).	**LET A = 4**
LIST	Lists specified lines or whole program. Space bar stops listing.	**LIST 100** **LIST** **LIST 50-80**
LLIST	Lists specified lines or whole program to printer.	**LLIST 100** **LLIST**
LN	Returns natural logarithm.	**A = LN(X − 2)**
LOG	Returns base ten logarithm.	**B = LOG(Y + 1)**
LORES N	Switches to low-resolution mode. TEXT screen is set to background black. When N = 0, the standard character set is used. When N = 1, the alternate character set is used.	**LORES 0**
MID$	Returns a substring starting at character A, of length L.	**A$ = MID$ (Z$,A,L)**
MUSIC	See Sound chapter.	
NEW	Deletes current program and all variables.	**NEW**
ON....GOSUB	Branches to subroutine at Nth line number specified.	**ON N GOSUB 2000,3000**
ON....GOTO	Branches to Nth line number specified.	**ON N GOTO 1000,2000**
PAPER	Changes background colour of whole screen. N is an integer 0-7.	**PAPER N**

PATTERN	Sets the pattern register for DRAW commands. X is an integer 0–255.	**PATTERN X**
PEEK	Returns the contents of memory location X.	**A = PEEK(X)**
PI	Returns the value 3.14159265.	**PRINT 2*PI**
PING	Produces predefined sound.	**PING**
PLAY	See Sound chapter.	
PLOT	Plots a character on the LORES or TEXT screen using X + Y co-ordinates.	**PLOT X,Y,"X"** **PLOT X,Y,A$**
POINT	Returns 0 if the specified pixel is background and − 1 if the pixel is foreground. X is absolute X value (0–239) Y is absolute Y value (0–199)	**POINT(X,Y)**
POKE	Stores value V in memory location N. V is an integer 0–255.	**POKE N,V**
POP	Causes one RETURN address to leave the stack of RETURN addresses. The next RETURN encountered after the POP branches to one statement beyond the second most recently executed GOSUB.	**POP**
POS	Returns the current horizontal position of the cursor.	**A = POS**
PRINT	Prints numbers, variables and strings on the screen. ? may be used instead of PRINT.	**PRINT "HELLO"** **PRINT N;A$**
PULL	Pulls one address from the stack in REPEAT loops. See POP.	**PULL**
READ	Reads next item in DATA list, and assigns it to specified variable.	**READ A$,N**
RELEASE	Assigns area described in GRAB command to the HIRES screen.	**RELEASE**
REM	Allows comments to be put in program lines. Everything after REM statement is ignored.	**REM IGNORE THIS**

REPEAT	Creates a loop to repeat all program lines up to UNTIL statement. Tests statement in UNTIL statement. If false, repeats loop. If true, continues execution at next program line.	
RESTORE	Sets READ pointer to first item on DATA lines.	**RESTORE**
RETURN	Returns the computer to the statement immediately after the most recent GOSUB.	**RETURN**
RIGHT$	Returns the right portion of a string, N characters in length.	**R$ = RIGHT$ (A$,N)**
RND	Returns a pseudo-random number. If X> = 1, then number is between Ø and 1 If X = Ø, then most recently generated number is produced. If X< Ø then number produced is the same for each X.	**A = RND(1)*6**
RUN	Executes a BASIC program from line N, or from lowest line if N is not specified. Also clears all variables.	**RUN 200**
SCRN(X,Y)	Returns the ASCII code for the character at position X,Y in LORES and TEXT modes.	
SGN	Returns − 1 if the argument is negative, Ø if zero and 1 if positive.	**Z = SGN(X − Y)**
SHOOT	Produces predefined sound.	**SHOOT**
SIN	Returns sine of angle N. N must be in radians.	**A = SIN(N)**
SOUND	See Sound chapter.	
SPC	Prints N spaces on the screen. N is an integer Ø−255.	**PRINT "HO" SPC(N) "HUM"**
SQR	Returns the square root of N.	**A = SQR(N)**
STOP	Stops execution of a program.	**STOP**
STR$	Converts a numerical expression into a string.	**N$ = STR$(N)**

TAB	Moves PRINT position N places from left of screen.	**PRINT TAB(N) "HELLO"**
TAN	Returns tangent of angle N. N must be in radians.	**A = TAN(N)**
TEXT	Switches to text mode.	**TEXT**
TROFF	Switches off trace function.	**TROFF**
TRON	Switches on trace function.	**TRON**
TRUE	Returns a value of − 1.	
USR	Passes value in brackets to a floating-point subroutine. See Chapter 13.	**USR(N)**
VAL	Returns the numerical value of string N$.	**A = VAL(N$)**
WAIT	Conditional pause. N = 10 msecs.	**WAIT (N)**
ZAP	Produces predefined sound.	**ZAP**

Appendix A

ORIC 1 MEMORY MAP (40K)

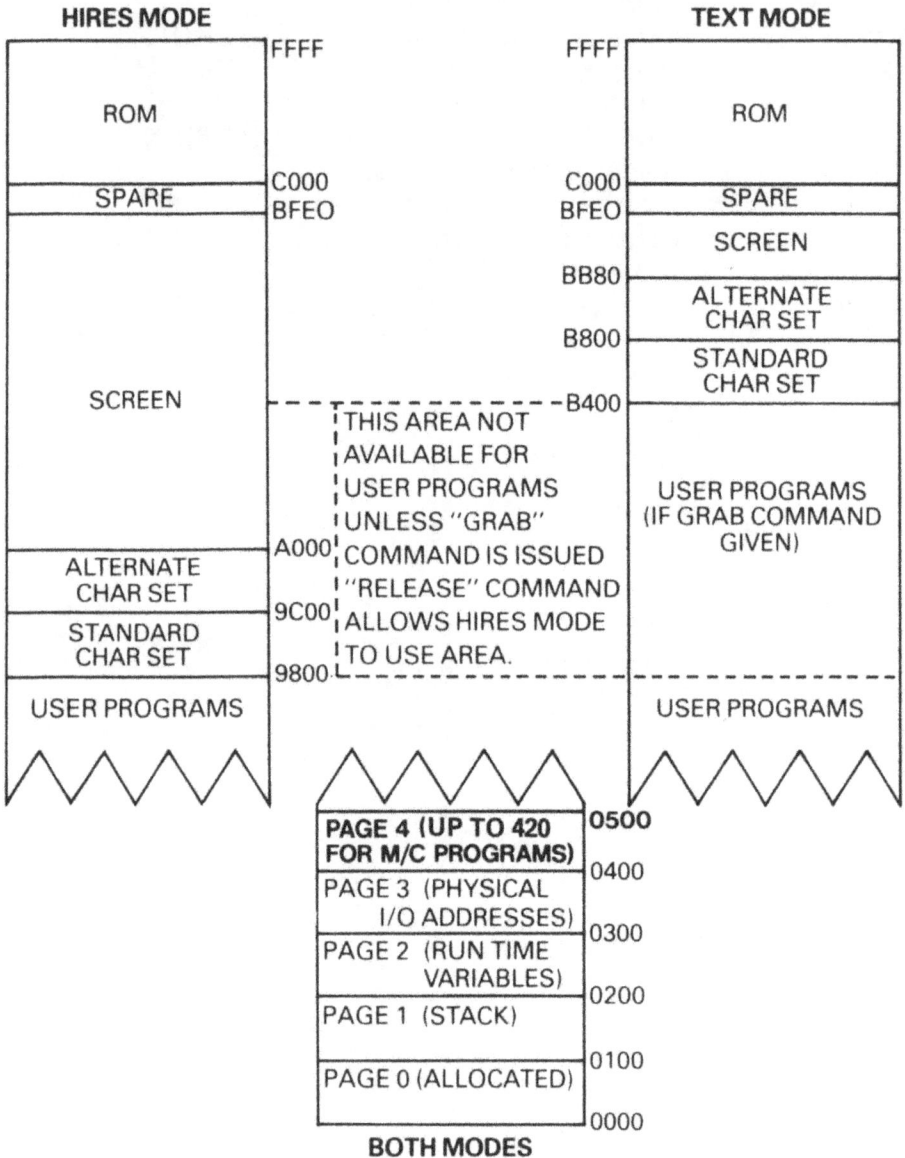

HIRES MODE

ROM	FFFF
SPARE	C000
	BFEO
SCREEN	
ALTERNATE CHAR SET	
STANDARD CHAR SET	
USER PROGRAMS	

TEXT MODE

ROM	FFFF
SPARE	C000
	BFEO
SCREEN	
ALTERNATE CHAR SET	BB80
STANDARD CHAR SET	B800
	B400
USER PROGRAMS (IF GRAB COMMAND GIVEN)	
USER PROGRAMS	

THIS AREA NOT AVAILABLE FOR USER PROGRAMS UNLESS "GRAB" COMMAND IS ISSUED "RELEASE" COMMAND ALLOWS HIRES MODE TO USE AREA.

A000
9C00
9800

BOTH MODES

PAGE 4 (UP TO 420 FOR M/C PROGRAMS)	0500
PAGE 3 (PHYSICAL I/O ADDRESSES)	0400
PAGE 2 (RUN TIME VARIABLES)	0300
PAGE 1 (STACK)	0200
PAGE 0 (ALLOCATED)	0100
	0000

N.B.
1) For 16K systems all addresses (except ROM) are minus 8000 (hex)
2) All addresses are given in Hexadecimal.

Appendix B

Control Characters — all available from the keyboard or through **PRINT** statements.

1. Toggle action on/off
CTRL T — Caps lock
CTRL P — Printer
CTRL F — Keyclick
CTRL D — Auto double height
CTRL Q — Cursor
CTRL S — V.D.U.
CTRL]— Protected column (far left)

2. Screen format characters
CTRL J — Line feed
CTRL L — Clear return
CTRL M— Carriage return
CTRL N — Clear row

To use in **Print** statements use

PRINT CHR$(x)

where **x** is a number, **A = 1**, **B = 2**, etc., e.g.

CTRL D = CHR$(4)

Appendix C

Attributes

	b6 = 0		b6 = 0	
	b5 = 0		b5 = 0	
	b4 = 0		b4 = 1	
b3 b2 b1 b0				
0	FGND BLACK	@	BGND BLACK	P
1	RED	A	RED	Q
2	GREEN	B	GREEN	R
3	YELLOW	C	YELLOW	S
4	BLUE	D	BLUE	T
5	MAGENTA	E	MAGENTA	U
6	CYAN	F	CYAN	V
7	WHITE	G	WHITE	W
8	SH/ST STD	H	TEXT 60HZ	X
9	SH/ST ALT	I	TEXT 60HZ	Y
A	DH/ST STD	J	TEXT 50HZ	Z
B	DH/ST ALT	K	TEXT 50HZ	{
C	SH/FL STD	L	GRA 60HZ	I
D	SH/FL ALT	M	GRA 60HZ	}
E	DH/FL STD	N	GRA 50HZ	~
F	DH/FL ALT	O	GRA 50HZ	←

50 Hz applicable in U.K.
60 Hz applicable in U.S.
Misuse may cause temporary loss of screen synchronization.

└─── escape character ───┘

```
SH  = SINGLE HEIGHT
DH  = DOUBLE HEIGHT
ST  = STEADY
FL  = FLASH
GRA = DOT GRAPHICS
STD = STANDARD CHARACTER SET
ALT = USER CHARACTER SET
```

Appendix D

A.S.C.I.I. CODES (decimal)

Code	Character	Code	Character
32	Space	79	O
33	!	80	P
34	"	81	Q
35	#	82	R
36	$	83	S
37	%	84	T
38	&	85	U
39	'	86	V
40	(	87	W
41	)	88	X
42	*	89	Y
43	+	90	Z
44	,	91	[
45	-	92	\
46	.	93	]
47	/	94	↑
48	0	95	£
49	1	96	©
50	2	97	a
51	3	98	b
52	4	99	c
53	5	100	d
54	6	101	e
55	7	102	f
56	8	103	g
57	9	104	h
58	:	105	i
59	;	106	j
60	<	107	k
61	=	108	l
62	>	109	m
63	?	110	n
64	@	111	o
65	A	112	p
66	B	113	q
67	C	114	r
68	D	115	s
69	E	116	t
70	F	117	u
71	G	118	v
72	H	119	w
73	I	120	x
74	J	121	y
75	K	122	z
76	L	123	{
77	M	124		
78	N	125	}

Appendix E

Binary/Hex/Decimal conversion table

DEC.	BINARY	HEX.	DEC.	BINARY	HEX.
0	00000000	00	30	00011110	1E
1	00000001	01	31	00011111	1F
2	00000010	02	32	00100000	20
3	00000011	03	33	00100001	21
4	00000100	04	34	00100010	22
5	00000101	05	35	00100011	23
6	00000110	06	36	00100100	24
7	00000111	07	37	00100101	25
8	00001000	08	38	00100110	26
9	00001001	09	39	00100111	27
10	00001010	0A	40	00101000	28
11	00001011	0B	41	00101001	29
12	00001100	0C	42	00101010	2A
13	00001101	0D	43	00101011	2B
14	00001110	0E	44	00101100	2C
15	00001111	0F	45	00101101	2D
16	00010000	10	46	00101110	2E
17	00010001	11	47	00101111	2F
18	00010010	12	48	00110000	30
19	00010011	13	49	00110001	31
20	00010100	14	50	00110010	32
21	00010101	15	51	00110011	33
22	00010110	16	52	00110100	34
23	00010111	17	53	00110101	35
24	00011000	18	54	00110110	36
25	00011001	19	55	00110111	37
26	00011010	1A	56	00111000	38
27	00011011	1B	57	00111001	39
28	00011100	1C	58	00111010	3A
29	00011101	1D	59	00111011	3B

DEC.	BINARY	HEX.	DEC.	BINARY	HEX.
60	00111100	3C	94	01011110	5E
61	00111101	3D	95	01011111	5F
62	00111110	3E	96	01100000	60
63	00111111	3F	97	01100001	61
64	01000000	40	98	01100010	62
65	01000001	41	99	01100011	63
66	01000010	42	100	01100100	64
67	01000011	43	101	01100101	65
68	01000100	44	102	01100110	66
69	01000101	45	103	01100111	67
70	01000110	46	104	01101000	68
71	01000111	47	105	01101001	69
72	01001000	48	106	01101010	6A
73	01001001	49	107	01101011	6B
74	01001010	4A	108	01101100	6c
75	01001011	4B	109	01101101	6D
76	01001100	4C	110	01101110	6E
77	01001101	4D	111	01101111	6F
78	01001110	4E	112	01110000	70
79	01001111	4F	113	01110001	71
80	01010000	50	114	01110010	72
81	01010001	51	115	01110011	73
82	01010010	52	116	01110100	74
83	01010011	53	117	01110101	75
84	01010100	54	118	01110110	76
85	01010101	55	119	01110111	77
86	01010110	56	120	01111000	78
87	01010111	57	121	01111001	79
88	01011000	58	122	01111010	7A
89	01011001	59	123	01111011	7B
90	01011010	5A	124	01111100	7C
91	01011011	5B	125	01111101	7D
92	01011100	5C	126	01111110	7E
93	01011101	5D	127	01111111	7F

Appendix F

Pin Output Chart

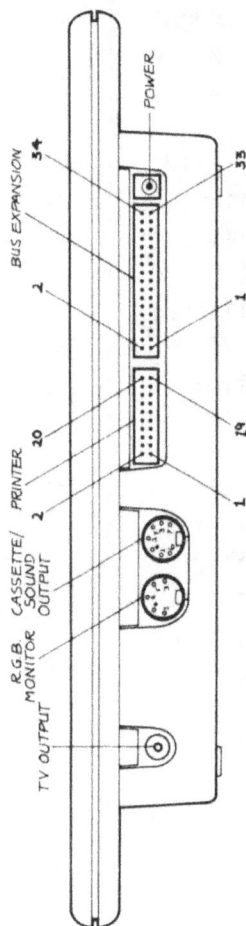

BUS EXPANSION

MAP	1	2	ROMDIS
Ø2	3	4	RESET
I/O	5	6	I/O Control
R/W	7	8	IRQ
D2	9	10	DØ
A3	11	12	D1
AØ	13	14	D6
A1	15	16	D3
A2	17	18	D4
D5	19	20	A4
A5	21	22	D7
A6	23	24	A15
A7	25	26	A14
A8	27	28	A13
A9	29	30	A12
A10	31	32	A11
+5V	33	34	GND

PRINTER

STB	1	2	GND
DO	3	4	GND
D1	5	6	GND
D2	7	8	GND
D3	9	10	GND
D4	11	12	GND
D5	13	14	GND
D6	15	16	GND
D7	17	18	GND
ACK	19	20	GND

R.G.B.

1 — RED
2 — GREEN
3 — BLUE
4 — SYNC
5 — GND

CASSETTE/SOUND

1 Tape Out
2 GND
3 Tape In
4 Sound 8912
5 Sound
6 Relay Contact
7 Relay Contact

Appendix G

Derived Functions

These functions are not directly available on Oric, but can be defined using **DEF FN**. e.g:

DEF FN SC(X) = 1/COS(X)

defines the secant.

Secant:
SEC(X) = 1/COS(X)

Cosecant:
CSC(X) = 1/SIN(X)

Cotangent:
COT(X) = 1/TAN(X)

Inverse sine:
ARCSIN(X) = ATN(X/SQR(−X*X + 1))

Inverse cosine:
ARCCOS(X) = −ATN(X/SQR(−X*X + 1)) + 1.5708

Inverse secant:
ARCSEC(X) = ATN(SQR(X*X − 1)) + (SGN(X) − 1)*1.5708

Inverse cosecant:
ARCCSC(X) = ATN(1/SQR(X*X − 1)) + (SGN(X) − 1)*1.5708

Inverse cotangent:
ARCCOT(X) = −ATN(X) + 1.5708

Hyperbolic sine:
SINH(X) = (EXP(X) − EXP(−X))/2

Hyperbolic cosine:
COSH(X) = (EXP(X) + EXP(−X))/2

Hyperbolic tangent:
TANH(X) = −EXP(−X)/(EXP(X) + EXP(−X))*2 + 1

Hyperbolic secant:
SECH(X) = 2/(EXP(X) + EXP(−X))

Hyperbolic cosecant:
CSCH(X) = 2/(EXP(X) − EXP(− X))

Hyperbolic cotangent:
COTH(X) = EXP(− X)/(EXP(X) − EXP(− X))*2 + 1

Inverse hyperbolic sine:
ARGSINH(X) = LOG(X + SQR(X*X + 1))

Inverse hyperbolic cosine:
ARGCOSH(X) = LOG(X + SQR(X*X − 1))

Inverse hyperbolic tangent:
ARGTANH(X) = LOG((1 + X)/1 − X))/2

Inverse hyperbolic secant:
ARGSECH(X) = LOG((SQR(− X*X + 1) + 1)/X

Inverse hyperbolic cosecant:
ARGCSCH(X) = LOG(SGN(X)*SQR(X*X + 1) + 1)/X

Inverse hyperbolic cotangent:
ARGCOTH(X) = LOG((X + 1)/(x − 1))/2

A Mod B:
MOD(A) = INT((A/B − INT(A/B))*B + 0.05)*SGN(A/B)

Appendix H

Text Screen Map

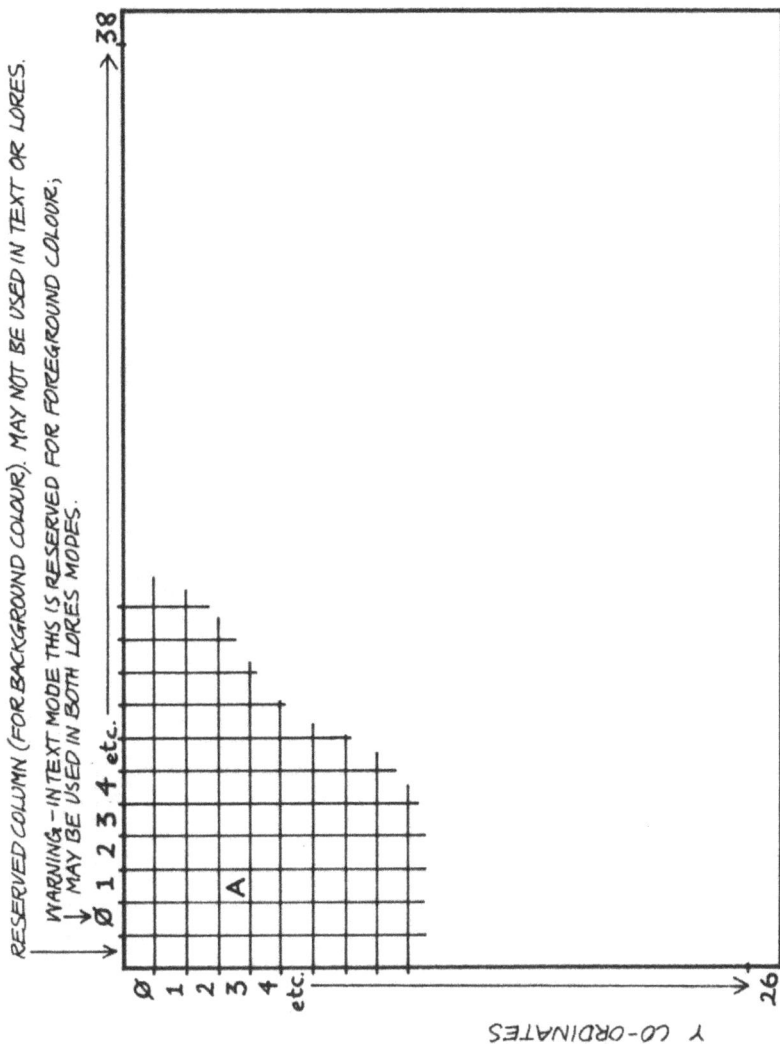

RESERVED COLUMN (FOR BACKGROUND COLOUR). MAY NOT BE USED IN TEXT OR LORES.

WARNING – IN TEXT MODE THIS IS RESERVED FOR FOREGROUND COLOUR; MAY BE USED IN BOTH LORES MODES.

Ø 1 2 3 4 etc.

A

Ø 1 2 3 4 etc.

38

26

X CO-ORDINATES

Y CO-ORDINATES

EXAMPLE :- PLOT 1,3, "A"
PLOTS AN A AS SHOWN

SCREEN MAP — TEXT, LORES Ø AND LORES 1 MODES.

Appendix I

High Resolution Screen Map

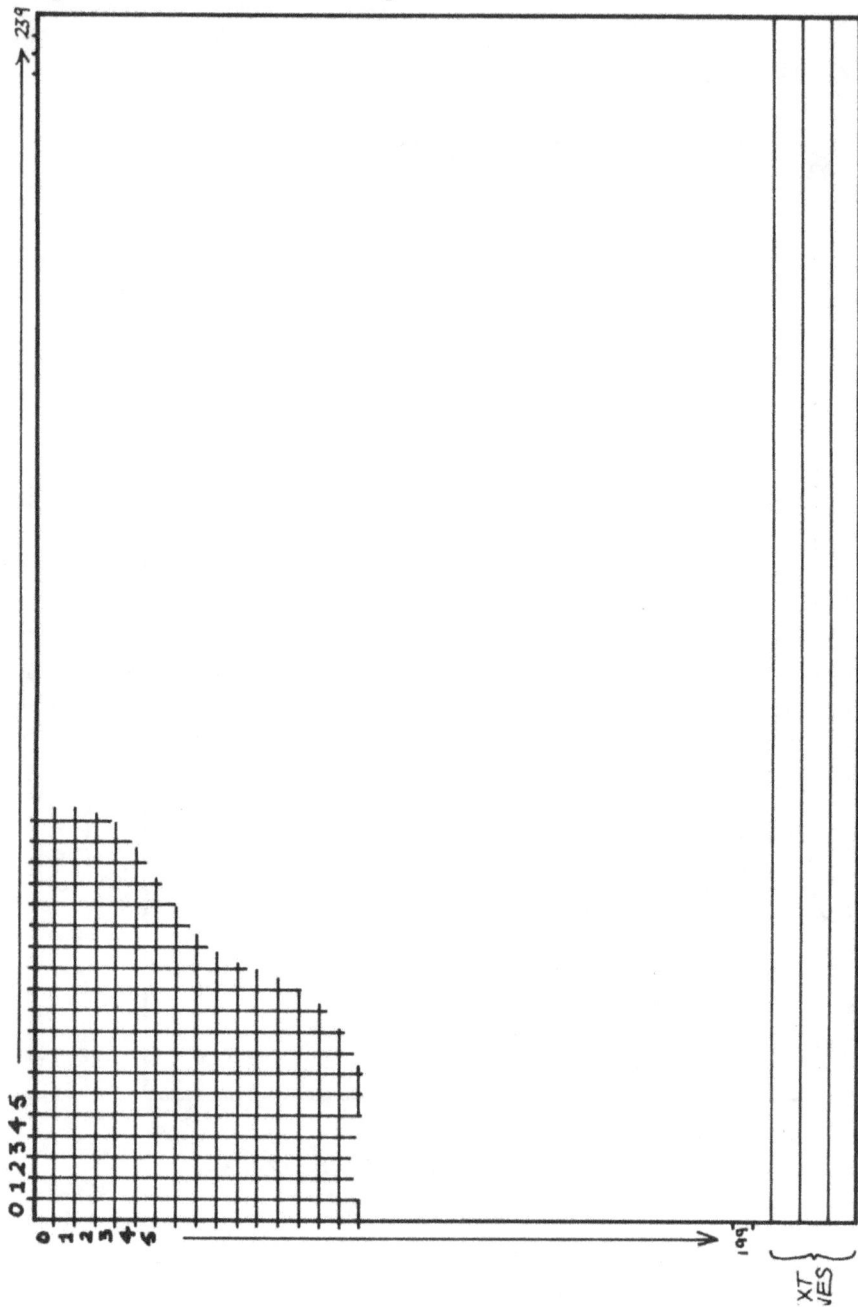

SCREEN MAP FOR HIRES MODE

Appendix J

If ORIC cannot handle a command or some information, then an error message will result. It will be followed by the line number where the error occurred if it was in a program. These are the possible codes and their meanings.

1.) **CAN'T CONTINUE**

   Attempt to continue a program after a line has been added or deleted.

2.) **DISP TYPE MISMATCH**

   Attempt to **DRAW** in **TEXT** mode or similar problem.

3.) **DIVISION BY ZERO**

   Difficult, even for ORIC!

4.) **FORMULA TOO COMPLEX**

   More than two **IF/THEN** statements in the same line.

5.) **ILLEGAL DIRECT**

   A statement such as **DATA** or **INPUT** has been used as a direct command from the keyboard.

6.) **ILLEGAL QUANTITY**

   Out of range parameter, e.g. $SQR(-1)$

7.) **NEXT WITHOUT FOR**

   Self-explanatory (one hopes!)

8.) **OUT OF DATA**

   Trying to **READ** past the end of the **DATA** list

9.) **OUT OF MEMORY**

   Self-explanatory, but might also be caused by more than 16 nested **FOR..NEXT/TO** loops or sub-routines.

10.) **OVERFLOW**

   A number larger than $1.70141*10^{38}$ has occurred during a calculation.

11.) **REDIM'D ARRAY**

   Attempt to redimension an array previously dimensioned.

12.) **RETURN WITHOUT GOSUB**

   Self-explanatory.

13.) **STRING TOO LONG**

Strings must be less than 255 characters in length.

14.) **BAD SUBSCRIPT**

An attempt has been made to reference an array element that does not exist. e.g. **LET A(24,25) = Z** when **A** has been dimensioned using **DIM A(4,4)**

15.) **SYNTAX ERROR**

Incorrect punctuation or missing bracket, etc.

16.) **TYPE MISMATCH**

An attempt has been made to assign a string to a numeric variable or vice versa.

17.) **UNDEF'D STATEMENT**

An attempt has been made to access a non-existent line number using GOTO, THEN or GOSUB.

18.) **UNDEF'D FUNCTION**

Attempt to use a function that has not been previously defined.

19.) **REDO FROM START**

Attempt to enter a string when a number was requested. Goes back to **INPUT**command.

20.) **BAD UNTIL**

Control has reached an **UNTIL** without previously encountering a **REPEAT** statement.

Appendix K

The 6502 monitor

PROCESSOR PROGRAMMING MODEL

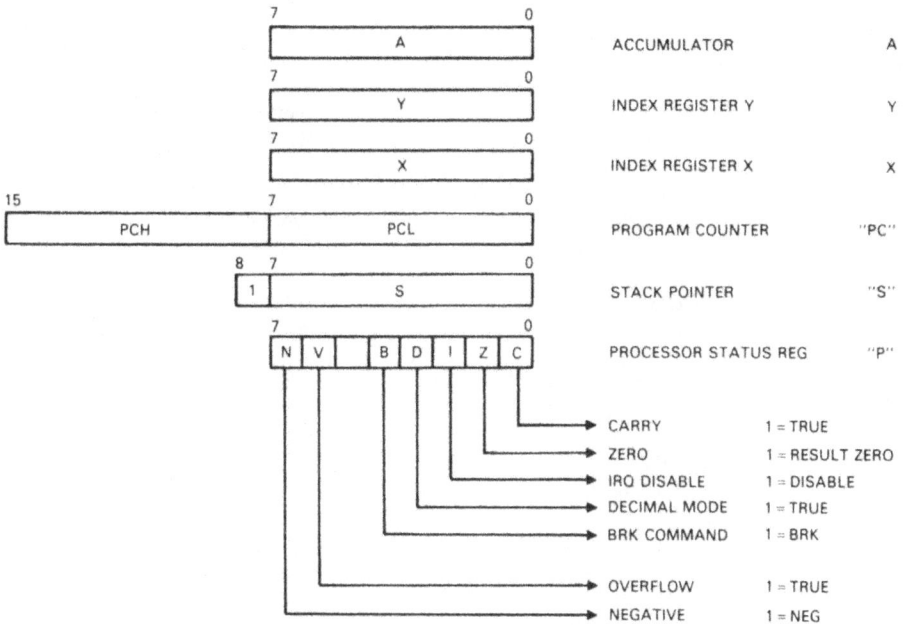

Register	Bits	Name	Symbol
A	7—0	ACCUMULATOR	A
Y	7—0	INDEX REGISTER Y	Y
X	7—0	INDEX REGISTER X	X
PCH / PCL	15—7—0	PROGRAM COUNTER	"PC"
1 / S	8—7—0	STACK POINTER	"S"
N V B D I Z C	7—0	PROCESSOR STATUS REG	"P"

CARRY   1 = TRUE
ZERO   1 = RESULT ZERO
IRQ DISABLE   1 = DISABLE
DECIMAL MODE   1 = TRUE
BRK COMMAND   1 = BRK

OVERFLOW   1 = TRUE
NEGATIVE   1 = NEG

MACHINE INSTRUCTIONS

ADC	Add Memory to Accumulator with Carry	LDX	Load Index X with Memory
AND	AND Memory with Accumulator	LDY	Load Index Y with Memory
ASL	Shift Left One Bit (Memory or Accumulator)	LSR	Shift Right One Bit (Memory or Accumulator)
BCC	Branch on Carry Clear	NOP	No Operation
BCS	Branch on Carry Set	ORA	OR Memory with Accumulator
BEQ	Branch on Result Zero	PHA	Push Accumulator on Stack
BIT	Test Bits in Memory with Accumulator	PHP	Push Processor Status on Stack
BMI	Branch on Result Minus	PLA	Pull Accumulator from Stack
BNE	Branch on Result Not Zero	PLP	Pull Processor Status from Stack
BPL	Branch on Result Plus	ROL	Rotate One Bit Left (Memory or Accumulator)
BRK	Force Break	ROR	Rotate One Bit Right (Memory or Accumulator)
BVC	Branch on Overflow Clear	RTI	Return from Interrupt
BVS	Branch on Overflow Set	RTS	Return from Subroutine
CLC	Clear Carry Flag	SBC	Subtract Memory from Accumulator with Borrow
CLD	Clear Decimal Mode	SEC	Set Carry Flag
CLI	Clear Interrupt Disable Bit	SED	Set Decimal Mode
CLV	Clear Overflow Flag	SEI	Set Interrupt Disable Status
CMP	Compare Memory and Accumulator	STA	Store Accumulator in Memory
CPX	COmpare Memory and Index X	STX	Store Index X in Memory
CPY	Compare Memory and Index Y	STY	Store Index Y in Memory
DEC	decrement Memory by One	TAX	Transfer Accumulator to Index X
DEX	Decrement Index X by One	TAY	Transfer Accumulator to Index Y
DEY	Decrement Index Y by One	TSX	Transfer Stack Pointer to Index X
EOR	Exclusive-OR Memory with Accumulator	TXA	Transfer Index X to Accumulator
INC	Increment Memory by One		
INX	Increment Index X by One	TXS	Transfer Index X to Stack Pointer
INY	Increment Index Y by One		
JMP	Jump to New Location	TYA	Transfer Index Y to Accumulator
JSR	Jump to New Location Saving Return Address		
LDA	Load Accumulator with Memory		

INSTRUCTION CODES

Name Description	Operation	Assembly Language Form	Addressing Mode	No. Bytes	HEX OP Code	Processor Status Reg. Codes.
ADC Add memory to accumulator with carry	$A \cdot M \cdot C \rightarrow A.C.$	ADC ⊣Oper ADC Oper ADC Oper.X ADC Oper ADC Oper.X ADC Oper.Y ADC (Oper.X) ADC (Oper).Y	Immediate Zero Page Zero Page.X Absolute Absolute X Absolute Y (indirect.X) (Indirect).Y	2 2 2 3 3 3 2 2	69 65 75 60 70 79 61 71	N V Z C
AND "AND" memory with accumulator	$A \Delta M \rightarrow$	AND ⊣Oper AND Oper AND Oper.X AND Oper AND Oper.X AND Oper.Y AND (Oper.X) AND (Oper).Y	Immediate Zero Page Zero Page.X Absolute Absolute.X Absolute.Y (Indirect.X) (Indirect).Y	2 2 2 3 3 3 2 2	29 25 35 20 30 39 31 31	N Z
ASL Shift left one bit (Memory or Accumulator)		ASL A ASL Oper ASL Oper.X ASL Oper ASL Oper.X	Accumulator Zero Page Zero Page.X Absolute Absolute.X	1 2 2 3 3	OA 06 16 OE 1E	N Z C
BCC Branch on carry clear	Branch on C = 0	BCC Oper	Relative	2	90	
BCS Branch on carry set	Branch on C = 1	BCS Oper	Relative	2	80	
BEQ Branch on result zero	Branch on Z = 1	BEQ Oper	Relative	2	FO	
BIT Test bits in memory with accumulator	$A \Delta M \; M_7 \rightarrow N.$ $M_6 \rightarrow V$	Bit* Oper BIT* Oper	Zero Page Absolute	2 3	24 2C	M_7, M_6, Z
BMI Branch on result minus	Branch on N = 1	BMI Oper	Relative	2	30	
BNE Branch on result not zero	Branch on Z = 0	BNE Oper	Relative	2	DO	
BPL Branch on result plus	Branch on N = 0	BPL Oper	Relative	2	10	
BRK Force Break	Forced Interrupt PC + 2 |P|	BRK*	Implied	1	00	$B, I \rightarrow 1$
BVC Branch on overflow clear	Branch on V = 0	BVC Oper	Relative	2	50	

Name Description	Operation	Assembly Language Form	Addressing Mode	No. Bytes	HEX OP Code	Processor Status Reg. Codes.
BVS Branch on overflow set	Branch on V = 1	BVS Oper	Relative	2	70	
CLC Clear carry flag	O→C	CLC	Implied	1	18	C→0
CLD Clear decimal mode	O→D	CLD	Implied	1	D8	D→0
CLI	O→1	CLI	Implied	1	58	I→0
CLV Clear overflow flag	O→V	CLV	Implied	1	88	V→0
CMP Compare memory and accumulator	A — M	CMP ⊣Oper CMP Oper CMP Oper.X CMP Oper CMP Oper.X CMP OPer.Y CMP (Oper.X) CMP (Oper).Y	Immediate Zero Page Zero Page.X Absolute Absolute.X Absolute.Y (Indirect.X) (Indirect).Y	2 2 2 3 3 3 2 2	C9 C5 D5 CD DD D9 C1 D1	N Z C
CPX Compare memory and Index X	X — M	CPX ⊣Oper CPX Oper CPX Oper	Immediate Zero Page Absolute	2 2 3	EO E4 EC	N Z C
CPY Compare memory and Index Y	Y — M	CPY ⊣Oper CPY Oper CPY Oper	Immediate Zero Page Absolute	2 2 3	CO C4 CC	N Z C
DEC Decrement memory by one	M — 1 →M	DEC Oper DEC Oper.X DEC Oper DEC Oper.X.	Zero Page Zero Page.X Absolute Absolute.X	2 2 3 3	C6 D6 CE DE	N Z
DEX Decrement Index X by one	X — 1 →X	DEX	Implied	1	CA	N Z
DEY Decrement Index Y by one	Y — 1 →Y	DEY	Implied	1	88	N Z

Name Description	Operation	Assembly Language Form	Addressing Mode	No. Bytes	HEX OP Code	Processor Status Reg. Codes.
EOR "Exclusive-OR" memory with accumulator	A V M→A	EOR ⊬Oper EOR Oper EOR Oper.X EOR Oper EOR Oper.X EOR Oper.Y EOR (Oper.X) EOR (Oper).Y	Immediate Zero Page Zero Page.X Absolute Absolute.X Absolute.Y (Indirect.X) (Indirect).Y	2 2 2 3 3 3 2 2	49 45 55 40 . 50 59 41 51	N Z
INC Increment memory by one	M + 1→M	INC Oper INC Oper.X INC Oper INC Oper.X	Zero Page Zero Page.X Absolute Absolute.X	2 2 3 3	E6 F6 EE FE	N Z
INX Increment index X by one	X + 1→X	INX	Implied	1	E8	N Z
INY Increment index Y by one	Y + 1→Y	INY	Implied	1	C8	N Z
JMP Jump to new location	(PC + 1)→PCL (PC + 2)→PCH	JMP Oper JMP (Oper)	Absolute Indirect	3 3	4C 6C	
JSR Jump to new location saving return address	PC + 2| (PC + 1)→PCL (PC + 2)→PCH	JSR Oper	Absolute	3	20	
LDA Load accumulator with memory	M →	LDA ⊬Oper LDA Oper LDA Oper.X LDA Oper LDA Oper.X LDA Oper.Y LDA (Oper.X) LDA (Oper).Y	Immediate Zero Page Zero Page.X Absolute Absolute.X Absolute.Y (Indirect.X) (Indirect).Y	2 2 2 3 3 3 2 2	A9 A5 B5 AD BD B9 A1 B1	N Z
LDX Load index X with memory	M →X	LDX ⊬Oper LDX Oper LDX Oper.Y LDX Oper LDX Oper.Y	Immediate Zero Page Zero Page.Y Absolute Absolute.Y	2 2 2 3 3	A2 A6 B6 AE BE	N Z
LDY Load index Y with memory	M →Y	LDY ⊬Oper LDY Oper LDY Oper.X LDY Oper LDY Oper.X	Immediate Zero Page Zero Page.X Absolute Absolute.X	2 2 2 3 3	AO A4 B4 AC BC	N Z

133

Name Description	Operation	Assembly Language Form	Addressing Mode	No. Bytes	HEX OP Code	Processor Status Reg. Codes.
LSR						N C
Shift right one bit (memory or accumulator)		LSR A	Accumulator	1	4A	N→0
		LSR Oper	Zero Page	2	46	
		LSR Oper.X	Zero Page.X	2	56	
		LSR Oper	Absolute	3	4E	
		LSR Oper.X	Absolute.X	3	5E	
NOP						
No operation	No operation	NOP	Implied	1	EA	
ORA						N Z
"OR" memory with accumulator	A V M →A	ORA ⊨Oper	Immediate	2	09	
		ORA Oper	Zero Page	2	05	
		ORA Oper.X	Zero Page.X	2	15	
		ORA Oper	Absolute	3	00	
		ORA Oper.X	Absolute.X	3	1D	
		ORA Oper.Y	Absolute.Y	3	19	
		ORA (Oper.X)	(Indirect.X)	2	01	
		ORA (Oper).Y	(Indirect).Y	2	11	
PHA						
Push accumulator on stack	A↓	PHA	Implied	1	48	
PHP						
Push processor status on stack	P ↓	PHP	Implied	1	08	
PLA						N Z
Pull accumulator from stack	A ↑	PLA	Implied	1	68	
PLP						**Restored**
Pull processor status from stack	P ↑	PLP	Implied	1	28	
ROL						N Z C
Rotate one bit left (memory or accumulator)		ROL A	Accumulator	1	2A	
		ROL Oper	Zero Page	2	26	
		ROL Oper.X	Zero Page.X	2	36	
		ROL Oper	Absolute	3	2E	
		ROL Oper.X	Absolute.X	3	3E	
ROR						N Z C
Rotate one bit right (memory or accumulator)		ROR A	Accumulator	1	6A	
		ROR Oper	Zero Page	2	66	
		ROR Oper.X	Zero Page.X	2	76	
		ROR Oper	Absolute	3	6E	
		ROR Oper.X	Absolute.X	3	7E	

Name Description	Operation	Assembly Language Form	Addressing Mode	No. Bytes	HEX OP Code	Processor Status Reg. Codes.
TXA Transfer index X to accumulator	X → A	TXA	Implied	1	8A	N Z
TXS Transfer index X to stack pointer	X → S	TXS	Implied	1	9A	
TYA Transfer index Y to accumulator	Y → A	TYA	Implied	1	98	N Z

135

Also Available

METEORIC

M

PROGRAMMING

For the ORIC·1

ORIC-1

JOHN VANDER REYDEN